T0358105

Make Your Property Dreams Come True

2022-23

Andrew Crossley

Cover design: Luke Harris

Internal images: Caroline Ward; KiCreative and Nicole Ellingham; Love Ginger Designs.

Layout and typesetting: Busybird Publishing

busybird
publishing

Busybird Publishing
2/118 Para Road
Montmorency, Victoria
Australia 3094
www.busybird.com.au

.

Contents

About this Book

This book takes you through the proven strategies and 7-step process that you must follow every time you purchase an investment property. The 7-step process can also assist greatly with purchasing a Principal Place of Residence (PPR).

It is based on my ground-breaking 'Blueprint to success'. The blueprint© was designed to act as an easy-to-follow process to help as many people as possible achieve more success with property purchase and investment.

Most Australians are destined to suffer in retirement, unless they seriously look at how they could self-fund their living standards in retirement, everyone needs a plan to better financial security through property.

You can obtain your free copy of this blueprint by going to

www.australianpropertyadvisorygroup.com.au/resources

and simply enter some details in order to access and download my blueprint. You will also have access to a 'readiness to invest' questionnaire and a very useful 'research checklist'.

Most investors get something wrong when buying a property, and often, owner occupiers allow emotion to impact on their purchase, potentially to their detriment, and when you look at why, 99% of the time, it's because they did not follow every one of the seven steps in this book.

If you follow these seven steps, for every property purchase, you can save yourself time and money, dramatically reduce risk, improve potential, and almost certainly eliminate stress, frustration and fear from the experience.

There are also 'MUST' follow rules scattered throughout this book.

What you gain will be similar to you being mentored through the process of not only knowing what to do when thinking about buying an investment property or a new home, but why you should consider investing in property.

Every successful investor assesses their situation and what they want to achieve. They establish a plan, and they follow it, taking action to implement the plan. A tailored plan is based on a client's current situation and their future goals, to then grow a well-balanced and affordable to maintain portfolio. A tailored plan can provide a more achievable outcome than just buying an investment property and hoping for the best or buying several properties without them being aligned to a client's specific circumstances. Every person has a goal to retire comfortably and to have options available to them even prior to retirement, whether to do volunteer work, travel more, cut back working hours etc.

Successful property buyers' undertake the required research and put in place appropriate finance strategies. They build a team around them to help them each step of the way toward their future income goals for retirement or an earlier retirement and/or to give them more options later in life, freeing up time being the main one. Every purchaser of a should, I believe consider the information in my book when buying their next home. Purchasing in a good street, a property with a good layout, no major defects, will grow more in value and be in demand in the future if ever it's sold is so beneficial. The more money you can make on your home when you sell, the more you have to upsize or buy in a better area perhaps.

The steps in this book should function together, and many parts of each step (chapter) can be used/implemented simultaneously. To assist in a property being purchased in as much of a stress-free manner as possible, always refer to this book and if you wish to have further assistance, because you don't have time to do it yourself, or you are afraid or concerned with doing it yourself, it is recommended you contact www.australianpropertyadvisorygroup.com.au (APAG) to work with you each step of the way.

Also, try www.Austpag.com.au for assistance with a mortgage to access any available equity in your home or for the purchase of another property, or simply a refinance with the aim of a better interest rate. Mortgage finance strategies are crucial to better manage your borrowing capacity.

The information, applicability and implementation of the material in this book is appropriate everywhere in Australia, many of my clients are up and down the eastern seaboard, so I have made use of examples based primarily on this part of Australia. The fundamentals remain the same.

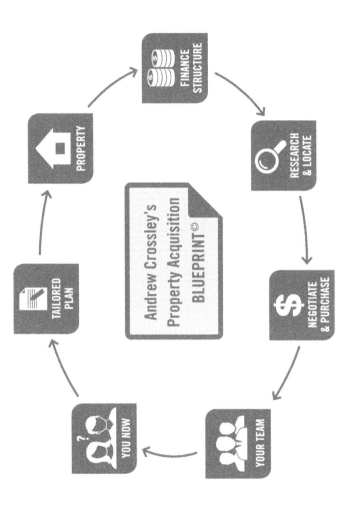

Your current situation

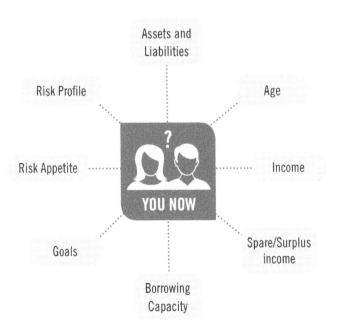

With anything you do of importance in life, it is far better to understand what you need to do before you try and do it. Without hope and goals we merely exist, there is nothing to strive for or look forward to.

Covid, though, was a period of mere existing rather than living unfortunately, but now we are past the worst of it, it would seem at this point time, hopefully 2019-2022 ended up being a time of reflection and progression of some sort in your life which you can leverage off now.

Impact on mental health has affected everyone to some degree I believe, it's how we can move forward that will define where we end up. Having a goal gives direction and purpose in life, be it a small or big goal, short term or long term.

Hopefully having made the most of the lock downs etc. as practicably as possible, now is time to reflect and leverage off anything positive that may have been achieved such some creative endeavour, self-discovery or financial betterment opportunity. I for one am over zoom and am also focused on losing the covid kilograms, I have found the Keto diet has really helped me, though this is not suitable for everyone.

Post Covid ...

Some things don't change. When it comes to buying a PPR, emotion is involved, yet it can benefit you to have a degree of commercial mindedness as well, such as preserving enough borrowing capacity, if possible, to purchase an investment property, even with a purchase price in the 300k-400k range.

In terms of property investment, your main goal should be a monetary one, NOT, 'I want 10 properties in 10 years'. This is foolish, and it lacks a practical outcome. The reason for the goal can be anything, such as a legacy, dream holiday or comfortable retirement.

In retirement, life comes down to survival, ideally living not just existing, and you need money for that. You will also need money for altruistic endeavours, giving back to society and leaving a greater legacy to your children.

A useful and considered outcome comes from determining your income requirement in retirement.

Retirement age can be open-ended; for some people it could be earlier in life than others. The younger someone starts investing, the more time for those assets to grow in value, and the more income potential will be derived from those assets in retirement.

Many people tend to assume that if they work hard and save money then one day, they will end up wealthy. This is wishful thinking for most people, as 80% will end up on the pension. With this mind-set, they are more likely to end up with a modest but ultimately less useful amount of savings.

They are unlikely to be wealthy unless they have their own business and sell it for a couple of million dollars. Some people are proud to have been a hard worker, I think it's better to have been a smart worker and successful in your career/ working life.

A useful goal is one that can be measured and has a chance of being achieved, and it should revolve around a passive income figure for retirement or working less at a younger age. An income figure could be $40,000 or $200,000 pa; what matters is that the figure is right for you.

Once you have a goal you will need to work backwards and knowing what you want and need in your retirement, it is easier to establish a plan of action. When you are still young and working, it is easier to leverage on your assets, in particular property, whilst not overstretching yourself. You still need to have a life.

Once you have a goal, you need to consider your current situation, adjust the goal as necessary. There is no point having a goal that is completely unachievable. What is achievable can often be more than what you might think, though, if you have a good team around you and a plan.

Income:

Your income will determine how much you can borrow. It also forms part of what you can afford to spend and save, and it impacts on what you can contribute to an investment property.

Income will help determine choice of property strategy. Less income may lead to the need for a regional location offering the benefit of greater yield (more focus on higher cash flow, to assist with borrowing capacity). A great income may mean a capital growth focused strategy is more viable and beneficial.

It is important to not be a slave to the cost of your debt, and to insure against rates rising or income changing, a balance of both capital growth and cash flow may therefore be a safer option than only a capital growth focus, depending on how negatively geared the properties are and the cost of the debt from an out-of-pocket perspective.

Assets and Liabilities:

The amount of debt you have will also impact on what you can borrow. The more credit cards you have, the worse off your borrowing capacity is. For every $1,000 of a credit card limit, it can negatively impact on borrowing capacity by up to or sometime over $5,000 borrowing capacity toward a mortgage.

Your age:

This can impact on your ability to obtain a loan, especially if you are over 55. The main impact from a property perspective is that it will directly impact how much time you have left to work and to achieve your 'passive income' goal for retirement.

It will also impact on the viable length of the plan moving forward, and the level of risk appropriate for your situation.

Lenders may start to show reticence in offering a 30-year loan term, and/or may offer 20-to-25-year loan term. Also, the lender may require Principal and Interest repayments on debt against the PPR, whilst debt secured against an investment property may be able to be interest only.

A feasible exit strategy would often be required. When it comes to exit strategy, the answer isn't to wipe out superannuation to pay off debt.

It isn't to downsize from, for example, a respectable suburb in metropolitan Melbourne to somewhere with a price far lower with a much lower socio demographic (which, could arguably lack a level of salubriousness that other suburbs possess, unless you have family there, then I hope you enjoy the move, and lenders will more likely consider this more acceptable. Downsizing shouldn't include sacrificing your current living standards too extremely.

Living expenses:

This impacts on the level of debt you can afford, your borrowing capacity, and the amount you can save. Lenders are placing an ever-increasing significance on this. In fact, besides your income, this is one of the greatest variables and it is studiously assessed, and every lender treats your living expenses differently. Savings and credit card account statements will be cross referenced to stated expenditure. Often people think they spend less than what they do, every lender and mortgage broker is required to cross reference stated living expenses with savings account, credit card account statements, and every account used for living expenses.

Notes should be provided around a one-off expense that may have appeared in the statements, which may have inflated the figure and cause a disparity to the living expense declaration form.

Not including private school fees will cause a non-disclosure allegation from the lender.

Smoking and drinking expense (people can be non-reality facing/embarrassed about the extent of their problem/addiction). Gambling (this could lead to a declined deal) depending on the gambling. Often expenses like rates/insurance/any owners corporation fees can be overlooked by the applicant for their PPR and particularly investment properties. Subscriptions is a big one, often people forget how many they have, some have subscriptions to several online streaming platforms.

Influences on living expenses

Suburb - Some lenders attribute greater living expenses to someone in a more expensive suburb like Double Bay or Toorak, compared to someone in a less expensive suburb like Blacktown, NSQ, Redbank Plains, Qld, or Werribee South, Vic.

People in more expensive suburbs have higher expenses. Their house is worth more, they often drive a more expensive car, and they spend more on entertainment, travel more etc.

There is an argument, the lender should go off actual expenses, however, there is a concern the applicant may just be trying to spend less immediately preceding applying for a loan, when in fact, their previous habits may show otherwise.

With rental costs, applicable if as an applicant for a loan you are renting, you may think that the person renting does not spend much because perhaps they live with their parents or rent for free, many lenders typically couldn't care less. Why?

One reason is the lender may not want to be complicit in effectively prohibiting that person from financially being able to move out of that rent free/low expense situation and on with their lives in a more independent fashion. The applicant (renter) in this case, could have a falling out with the person providing rent free accommodation.

Lenders generally cannot expect a person to live off their parents or a friend's generosity forever, nor should a lender provide a mortgage relying on this presumption that the applicant will continue to live rent free or continue to have few or no responsibilities.

Surplus/spare money:

This will contribute to what the plan needs to look like, and what is possibly achievable, it helps you sleep at night and more likely save as well as grow a buffer for emergencies. If you need to purchase a capital growth focused property, then often by default it will be negatively geared, traditionally anyway. Some regional areas are now recognized as capital growth locations, and they have excellent rental income. You would need to afford the higher out-of-pocket cost associated with capital growth focused suburbs

Don't be misguided in to buying property in Queensland (Qld) thinking blindly that it is good for positive cash flow. The councils in Qld, the insurance providers for Qld charge obscene amounts/premiums. Rental managers charge more than many other States, sales agents, if you ever sell charge approx. 0.7- 1%+ more than in Victoria for example. All these costs erode the higher rents. Northern Territory agents' commissions range up to 4%. On average across Australia its 2-3%.

The Government has now intentionally made it more difficult for you to afford to buy an established (already built and lived in) property, given you can no longer claim <u>any</u> depreciation on *any* fixtures and fittings that came with the property.

Very importantly, there are far too many people that have invested in property that have made the mistake of investing in high priced properties, or several properties, or simply taken on considerable debt for their circumstances, without adequate regard for the future cost of the debt. As rates rise, cost of debt rises, many people will be caught out.

Fixed rates are not your saviour, they simply provide stable repayments for a period, not better repayments in the long run, say over 20 years, anecdotally, it all works out the same compared to variable rates.

Interest only is not the answer for every person either. Over the life of the loan, you will pay more interest on the debt than if the repayments were principal and interest.

Yes, it may cost less in the short term of course than having principal and interest and can work well for many people to help them buy property and focus on reducing their own home loan that may not be providing any tsax benefits.

However, lenders have limits of time on how long, i.e., 1-5 years typically, that you can have interest only, some lenders may be reluctant to offer interest only rates when the borrower is older than 50 or 55 years of age, many lenders won't provide interest only loans for investment purpose debt secured against the PPR, when the borrower is of a certain age. This is not discrimination for the altruistic people out there, this is common sense, it is responsible lending. When you reach a certain age, it is important to be in a debt reduction phase of life, not a debt accumulation or non-debt reduction stage.

Additionally, the risk with having too much debt on interest only is that eventually you may be forced to pay principal and interest repayments, repayments then will be higher, perhaps around the vicinity of 40% higher. Many investors struggle when this happens. Having a phased approach to debts converting to principal and interest is always worth considering, it helps prevent too much debt converting to principal and interest at the same time, less of a shock.

Risk appetite and profile:

Investing involves risk. Risk is the chance that an investment will not give you the returns you hoped for. You could lose money or not make any money. All investments have risk, but some have more than others.

Generally, investments that are expected to pay higher returns involve more risk. These investments are more likely to produce higher returns over time than more conservative investments. Over short periods of time investments can fall in value. Property is a long-term, not short-term investment, unless you plan to develop or renovate the property. With a buy and hold strategy, it's certainly a longer-term strategy.

Your risk profile when determining a property plan is not designed to determine if you should invest in property or another asset, it's used to determine the strategy within the scope of property investment. Each type of strategy, location and property has its own risks and benefits. Your risk profile can be used to assist with trying to choose a strategy and property more suited to you, based on current situation, risk appetite, and future goals.

If you want a positive cash flow property this tends to suit lower risk appetites, preferring not to take the risk of being too negatively geared or the risk of waiting 10-15 years for a good income to come from it. Perhaps your health or job security is such that you prefer not to be out of pocket too much.

Capital growth strategies traditionally require a slightly higher risk appetite as you must wait for the growth, whilst earning less from the property.

This has changed recently, however. Since Covid, significant upward pressure in certain regional locations, and parts of Qld, have been unprecedented, whereby what used to be just a higher 'gross' cash flow focused strategy has become both capital growth and good cash flow in a number of good regional areas, though in Qld, whilst on the surface, the yields are great, I would not put this in the basket of good cash flow, as mentioned earlier, unless perhaps you had a good and subject to being suitable to your needs, a dual key/ dual occupancy or multi-generational family type property, or perhaps some NDIS type properties.

Some people may be more aggressive or assertive in how they wish to move forward, sometimes from desperation, or out of sheer necessity. However, a plan forward needs to be justified and responsible and managing your expectations. Sometimes a 'risk appetite' does not correlate to a 'risk profile'. For example, a couple who has more than 4-5 credit cards are a higher risk profile but may have a very low risk appetite when it comes to investment.

Some 'would be' property investors have a higher risk appetite than what they should have for their circumstances. This can end up putting them in a precarious situation, being exposed to too much debt, and possibly an untenable future cost of debt., especially when interest rates rise and their loans convert to principal and interest repayments, or their income changes, or living expenses rise.

Needs will vary depending on experience, knowledge and risk profile. Less experienced buyers generally want someone to manage the process for them and help them find a property.

RULE:

Always have a SMART goal. It must be specific, measurable, attainable, relevant to you and focused on a fixed point in time.

To fill in a readiness to invest questionnaire, please go to:

www.australianpropertyadvisorygroup.com.au/resources

In Summary:

Your age, income, borrowing capacity, living expenses, surplus money, risk profile, capital growth, rental incomes, competition in the market, will all have a bearing on the plan, and the reality and likelihood of the outcome (viability of your goal). Compromises may need to be made.

No two people will have the same strategy – it may be similar, but not the same. Your future is in your hands to a large enough degree for you to need to own it. Be responsible for it so that you can enjoy your future, just as you intended or hoped it to do. Don't risk having regrets and don't be one of those people that recite in their 70's I shoulda, coulda, woulda. If the opportunity isn't there, so be it, but if it is and it's ignored then what a waste.

Tailored Plan

Fear, not purchasing well, not building a large enough property portfolio, or simply just buying a property or two with no idea what the properties should be, also all affect a goal being achieved.

An intelligent investor will not just focus on capital growth. They want to avoid the risk of becoming overwhelmed with the debt in their portfolio, to have to keep working just to make repayments thinking they will wake up in 10 years and the portfolio has doubled in value. They want to sleep at night as interest rates rise (and rates are and will continue to be increased independently of the cash rate movement initiated by the Reserve Bank of Australia (RBA). May/June 2022, with inflation being at 5.1% was a turning point, post covid.

An intelligent investor will not focus just on positive cash flow either, as they want to achieve capital growth and more wealth by retirement. Whilst they don't want their properties to be a negative impact on their lifestyle, they realise the importance of capital growth.

Too many authors of property investment books, and others that operate within the property industry, promote just one strategy: either capital growth in blue chip suburbs or positive cash flow in regional locations. This is narrow minded. Why?

The most optimal plan is to buy several capital growth properties with good cash flow in blue chip suburbs near major infrastructure hubs, preferably near Melbourne or Sydney CBD, Hobart, parts of South Australia and specific locations in Qld, emphasis on specific locations in Qld, far too much of Qld is untenable to be considered investment grade security.

The reality is not everyone can afford to do this. The idealists out there who promote only buying capital growth properties in blue chip suburbs, or only buying positive cash flow focused properties, are just that – they are idealists, not realists. Their logic, in isolation to most people's financial situations, is sound, but it is disconnected from the vast reality of society in general, of typical mum and dad investors in the burbs.

Good capital growth locations typically have lower yield. This would mean the property would more likely be negatively geared.

Cash flow focused properties are often in areas with less capital growth, (holiday locations with the property on Airbnb is an obvious exception).

At least this strategy reduces the risk of being exposed too much to the unknown future cost of debt because the rental income is higher and purchase price lower. With the exception, buying in a holiday destination in Australia and having the property on Airbnb can be very lucrative. If you accept that it's not rented with a reliable income throughout the year, you could make much much more than a standard twelve-month lease. I help my clients with what they can do to a property like this in their portfolio to improve their potential income.

> **RULE:**
> *Investors typically need a balance of both capital growth and cash flow in order to grow a portfolio and more likely achieve their goal. A balance in enhancing borrowing capacity whist also wealth creation and growing equity more rapidly in their properties.*

Most investors do not earn enough to afford to purchase 5-7 properties in expensive blue-chip suburbs without regard for cash flow from those properties. Most people do not earn 200k+ a year, their job stability is not 10 out of 10, they do have some, or considerable fear, and lack knowledge, time and experience. People need help to invest in a practical way to suit them and their specific needs, not an ideological single strategy fashion, bereft of suitability and sustainability to them. Each property should complement each other property a person owns.

Cash flow properties are not necessarily wealth creation properties. They do, however, provide greater income while you are growing your portfolio, therefore allowing a property investor an increased capacity to continue to borrow, at the very least it positively impacts on borrowing capacity and helps supplement your living expenses. If the focus is only on capital growth properties, the ability to continue to borrow money will diminish, ultimately; they would run out of income to service the loans.

If an investor could no longer borrow money, it would not matter how much equity they have, as they'd be unable to access it unless significant amounts were already in redraw, or they had big cash reserves or shares they could cash in. If a person borrows their maximum to buy in the best area they can afford, they will diminish their ability to invest elsewhere. When I purchased where I live, it preserved my borrowing capacity rather than it being the best place I could afford to live. Still a great area with predominantly good neighbours, schools, transport and amenities, and great capital growth. If it isn't producing an income, it's a liability until its sold, even then it's a liability unless it's made an excellent profit.

It would be too easy, and very wrong to base a retirement decision on just one property. There are several considerations to bear in mind. Besides your exposure to the future cost of debt and receiving tax deductions, affordability to purchase more properties – whilst enabling you to continue to reduce your mortgage on your home – is very important. Combined, they provide hope; hope toward a brighter retirement, having done something rather than nothing.

The risk with only a capital growth strategy is the amount the borrower could be out of pocket while holding the properties. In a rising interest rate market (interest rates for investment loans) the risk grows.

There's no point buying a capital growth focused property if there is a clear and present risk that in the near future the property will need to be sold. Job uncertainty, tightening lending policies, lower borrowing capacity and risk of having to sell the property due to unforeseen circumstances, rising living costs and interest rates, is much higher. Changes to negative gearing are already problematic with established properties.

Lenders used to account for borrower's existing debt with other lenders by using actual repayments to determine the borrower's cost of debt. On an interest only loan of 500k in 2016, the repayments might have been $22,500 pa.

Now, lenders are adding a buffer on top of the borrowing capacity calculator and converting the interest only repayments to a figure based on principal and interest, as they do for the new loan being applied for.

The same 500k debt in 2022 would have a paper cost on the borrowing capacity associated to it of circa $41,500 pa. Again, based not just on a higher qualifying rate, but also principal and interest repayments, even though the investor may be paying interest only.

This is $19,000 more in income the borrowers need to have to afford the same debt on a bank's calculator as they previously could have.

Imagine they only purchased capital growth properties and none of them were cash flow focused properties, the strife this investor would be in, and on two main fronts.

Not being able to borrow as much and/or,

Maybe being forced to sell one or more, due to rising rates, and rising holding cost of debt.

Many investors over the years have been drawn to negative gearing, yet it makes little financial sense why these people were. Of course, they think they are saving a great deal of tax but let's put this into perspective.

According to the ATO, not too long ago, over 70% of investors that had a negatively geared property (a property not breaking even or not making positive cash flow) earned under 80k per annum. So, their tax bracket was mid-range, not high, or the highest. So, it is foolish to spend a dollar just to save 32.5 cents in the dollar, and this is what *all* these people (in that %). Sure, as a biproduct of investing, tax benefits are useful, this should never be the focus though.

There are three strategies for property investors.

Capital growth and cash flow strategies can be implemented in all three. The difference between the three of them is level of risk, time available to retirement, time in your day to be involved, knowledge, your tailored plan, comfort level, and many other influences.

1. Buy and hold

This is perhaps the easiest of the three strategies. It is more suited to time poor investors that wish to be a little more conservative, or that lack the knowledge and expertise to risk undertaking one of the other two strategies. Buy and hold is what most investors decide on.

Many still fail with this for innumerable reasons. Lack of knowledge and experience, poor research, not using an advisor, bad financial strategy, no plan, selling too early, buying at the wrong time in the wrong market, or buying the wrong property type in a good/average/bad suburb, to name a few.

2. Flipping

This requires a more hands-on approach or paying a premium to have someone renovate for you. The purchaser can manufacture more capital growth and cash flow independently of the market, so they're not solely reliant on the market for the property's performance.

If too much emotion is involved and they over-capitalise, serious problems will arise. Having it vacant for an extended period while work is being carried out means being out of pocket for a period of time.

Affordability could then be an issue, as it is more difficult to afford to have a property vacant for an extended period.

3. Develop

This includes construction of another dwelling or several dwellings on the block, and/or subdivision. This is the most risky, due to time and cost, but has potential for significantly more financial benefits from a cash flow and capital growth perspective. A feasibility study would be required to determine if the project will make enough money or will lose money.

You will also need a good team around you. Refer to www.propertyinvestingmadesimple. com.au to get an idea of who would be needed in your team for this type of investment. Also 'The 100k Property Plan' and 'Commercial Property and Residential Development Made Simple' where I go into significant detail on most things to do with small-scale developments.

With every plan, there are also three stages ...

An acquisition phase:

This is the period over which you acquire the required properties. It can be as short or long as is practical but needs to suit your current situation and all the elements of what makes up your current situation discussed in chapter 1.

The holding phase:

This is the period that you hold your properties. The longer this phase, with a buy and hold strategy, the more time the properties have available to grow in value.

Many property-marketing companies will tell you that property has doubled in value every 7-10 years and whilst this is true in many areas, what many of these people do wrong is imply that property will continue to double the next 7-10 years. They may not say it explicitly, but they often lead you to believe the chances of it are very high.

This I disagree with; the past is not a reliable indicator of the future. To be more reasonable with timeframes and in order to manage expectations, it is more reliable to allow 15 years, or even 20 years is better. Not everyone has this much time, and it is a sad fact of life that people often leave it too late in life to act for the betterment of their future.

What can be done for people who are young enough (not too old), is to consider starting now if their current situation allows it. The age for being young enough or not too old is subjective, depending on their circumstances. Generally, someone over 60, with no investment properties may have left it too late. For those people who have left it late to attain all their future aspirations, they could consider whether they should start now, to at least try and improve their situation, seek advice at least.

The older someone becomes, the more conservative they should consider being. They have less time to try and mitigate any financial mistakes they make, less time available in their working life to make repayments.

Exit phase:

There are a few favoured exit strategies. It is best to seek advice from a property advisor for a tailored approach.

1. Sell some and pay off the debt on the rest leaving the remaining properties hopefully unencumbered. This works when there are more than just a few properties, and some with a capital growth focus. You may or may not have reduced some of the debt. The less debt you want to reduce, the more confidence you would need with the market.

2. Reduce debt, assisted by perhaps an offset account and principal and interest (P & I) repayments on any mortgage secured against the PPR. Firstly, focus on the debt not providing any tax benefit. Once non-deductible debt is paid off, then a person may consider an offset against the deductible debt secured against the PPR, or investment property, originally used for deposit and costs of a property purchase.

3. A blend of 1 and 2 may suit some, subject to affordability, household cash flow etc.

4. Live off equity in retirement. Prior to retiring, apply to refinance all properties, setting up redraw against some or all. Using equity to live off is different to earning income to live off, as it is not taxed.

5. Sell all properties. Hopefully walk away with a great amount in equity, then purchase a few properties with high yield, for example 10% and live off the rent. Understand the capital gains tax ramifications of course. Also, and critically, *anything you claimed*

in depreciation while you owned the investment property must be paid back to the ATO, if you sell. Terrible isn't it, but true, depreciation is nice to help afford holding onto the investment property, but it comes back to bite you later, if you sell. A PPR is different. Speak to your accountant.

Example: If your home, or an investment property, had enough equity to establish an offset or redraw facility against it of $400k (could be more or less, but let's say $400k), just before retirement, while still earning assumedly sufficient income to service this amount, then…. the undrawn equity could sit in the loan not incurring interest, it saves interest. It could provide $40k pa to live off for 10 years, which would put the borrower closer to the highest percentage of retired income earners in Australia.

Let's assume, in this example, superannuation and any additional shares provided an income of $15k pa. Only $25k needs to be used from the loan facility secured against any properties, to possibly earn $40k per year, meaning, if there was $400k in an 'appropriate to your circumstances' loan facility, it could last for 16 years.

Imagine having a couple of properties with access to $400k equity in each.

Note: point number four is one some others promote. It has, as a concept, been around for 20 years, but often these people fail to adequately explain the mechanics and downside of it. Some reasons it may be problematic are:

Accessing equity after retirement is very difficult and unlikely possible, as lenders will need the borrower to have enough income to service an increase in the existing debt level, and an acceptable exit strategy.

Lending policy may inhibit further borrowing; you cannot rely on what lenders will do in five, or twenty-five years. Additionally, it is not always so easy to refinance just when the borrower wants to.

We will eventually die, leaving all the debt-covered properties to someone else. This would be unfortunate and not considered a welcomed legacy.

Some elderly decide on a reverse mortgage, and this can have serious consequences. It's one of the more expensive forms of debt, if you speak to a suitably qualified professional, they may tell you, that this could impact on the person's ability and ease to be able to afford aged care, and/or pension eligibility. Best to seek appropriate advice.

In summary:

The type of property strategies and the number of properties of each strategy will impact on location choice, and therefore outcome. Between 5-7 well purchased properties is better than just choosing a number like 10 as a naïve goal for a portfolio.

Even 2 properties are better than doing nothing in one's life toward their future, other than Superannuation. Property advisors do have software to model outcomes using conservative assumptions of growth and yield figures, using conservative figures is very important as this is less likely to mis-manage expectations.

It is important that someone doesn't just buy and then sit and wait. They need to review their plan, portfolio, goals based on any changes to their circumstances, and the performance of the property and the market which it's in. It means that if the portfolio performs better, what had been planned for may be exceeded. If it does not perform as well as anticipated, at least modelled figures have been conservative to begin with, properties may perhaps need to be offloaded, though, if you had sought advice this is far less likely. A risk tolerance review is also important.

Reducing debt that provides tax deductions is not the best approach if there is debt that does not provide you tax deductions, but it does have other longer-term benefits, which need to be weighed up, and which I mentioned earlier.

Whilst any applicable depreciation on the dwelling is on a straight-line method at 2.5% each year over 40 years, depreciation on fittings and fixtures, if applicable, does diminish over the short term (on average 7-15 years), so the cost of debt will increase accordingly as any benefits of depreciation diminish on the fixtures and fittings, (this is not a problem with having purchased an established/pre-owned property-no depreciation allowed). What assists in the debt not increasing much is rental increasing at the same rate of knots, as the diminishing of any fixtures and fittings depreciation.

To help mitigate this rise in cost of debt (to help weather the storm of rising rates) especially on interest only and investment loans, and to maximum the difference between the value of the property and level of debt and make it more cash flow positive (if you can afford to), a debt reduction strategy is generally wise, working in with the reduction of any debt not associated with investment.

The bigger picture is the focal point, in a managed manner of course, but if you significantly reduce your debt over time, it will lessen the debt ultimately against your properties and perhaps reduce the number of properties you may need to sell. It's very important to consider principal and interest repayments on the properties at the appropriate time.

> ### RULE:
>
> *Please remember you will probably have to convert your repayments to principal and interest at some point, which in turn will reduce your debt. The more debt you do reduce, the better the outcome in the end, as long as you can afford to do this.*

Sadly, any depreciation claimed will need to be paid back to the Government if you sell.

You need capital growth for wealth creation.

This can provide the equity which may be accessed to use for the deposit and costs of buying more properties and paying off debt on other properties nearer retirement leaving a final number unencumbered is the most appealing outcome.

Paul Clitheroe from *Money Magazine* proposes a multiple of 17. Work out what you need in retirement, and then multiply it by 17, this is what you will apparently need. He suggests that 17 is the years you will live beyond retirement. If you live beyond that, well, you are possibly in trouble. If you retire too early, then you may also be in trouble. For some people a perfect outcome is to have had a good retirement, and die having spent their last dollar, not ideal for many others who wish to bequeath monies and other assets.

A plan's focus is to acquire an appropriate number of properties for your specific needs, over a given time, at a given price, to achieve a desired passive income – all within an appropriate risk tolerance and level of affordability throughout the entire process.

It is worth reiterating that a plan is better than not having a plan at all. If you fall short, well, you would have achieved more than not having a plan to begin with.

My book 'The 100k Property Plan' goes much more in-depth and provides an example of tailored plan based on a reasonably common avatar (2 adults and 2 kids).

3

Property Strategy

Once you have a plan of action, it is important to determine the type of properties that best suit the chosen path forward. It is of course of underlying importance to factor in your PPR if you have one, if you 'rentvest' then good also.

Often people tie up a considerable amount of their borrowing capacity into their home, this can be good and bad. It can be good because the PPR can often become the cash cow, the equity provider for deposits toward investment properties. As investment properties grow in value, the investments themselves can provide the equity for future deposits. Ultimately it doesn't matter where equity comes from.

It can be bad because it may limit the ability to borrow enough for another property. With risk of going off on a tangent here, far too often I become aware of people who have a bit of a façade going on, they buy in an area to project a perception they want others to have of them, by maxing themselves out in the process (keep up with the Jones). They may buy a fancy car under finance (often the case); expensive cars are the first thing that goes when times get tough. Personally, I think it so important to avoid owing money on a credit card beyond the 55 days interest free period, it's dangerous to borrow too much for a car also.

Often a car is a liability, not an asset, according to Robert Kiyosaki in his famous book 'Rich Dad Poor Dad', anything that doesn't make you money is a liability, so to borrow for a liability is perhaps counter intuitive, this may extend to the PPR to some degree, even though it may be growing very well in value, it certainly isn't providing an income.

Scarily, a friend who works as a debt collector mentioned in passing the most common debt being chased is where people have failed miserably to maintain the private school tuition fees.

Again, it's important to not live beyond one's means. It may not necessarily be in the present, based on their present situation, that someone decides to spend too much, it is often during 'blind hope' things will be better, and she'll be right mate attitude, they think they can afford it, or often without sufficient regard for potential negative impacts to their job, health, income etc., which they have been ill-prepared for.

Psychologically, some people want to remove the house from the equation of taking out more debt against it, but debt is debt, however you cut it, it doesn't matter how its secured, provided repayments are always met.

If a person is in default of their repayments, the lender can eventually repossess the property, perhaps some people are afraid of this. Debt against the home can lead to a cheaper rate with one or two lenders. Most lenders price the interest rate on the purpose of the debt, whereas a fewer number of lenders price (offer a better rate) based on the security (property) used for the debt.

Importantly, speak to your accountant about redraw versus offset, not good to have 'redraw' against an investment property purpose debt, your accountant may suggest an offset is better.

If you save money in a redraw against an investment purpose debt, it will muddy the waters with the balance of the investment purpose debt rising and falling as money is put in and taken out, causing issues later at tax time, as you put money in and take money out you cannot beneficially change what you claim from an interest perspective as a tax deduction. For example, you have 100k of investment debt, and you put 10k in of savings, the debt is now 90k that the borrower would pay interest on, then let's say 5k of the savings is spent, the debt that interest is paid on is now 95k, however, the tax deductible interest is still based on 90k. What a person claims cannot go up and down. Offset is different, whereby the debt remains unimpacted by any monies in the offset account.

The order in which you implement the plan will be clear if it's well written.

The first choice you need to make is between residential and commercial property. This book will focus more on residential.

RULE:

Negative gearing is NOT a strategy; never focus on buying a negatively geared property.

To reiterate, negative gearing is, and should be, simply only a bi-product of a property purchase that is not cash flow positive, more commonly referred to as a bi-product of a capital growth focused strategy or sadly, an apartment in Qld and some parts of some other States, Qld being the biggest culprit of a property ending up being negatively geared, where insurance premiums, and owner's corporation fees lead to the property often being negatively geared. Don't just compare the rent versus the mortgage, that's not very smart, look at all the costs.

If you have any bad habits when counting calories, don't let these creep into property investment, i.e., if you eat a pie with ketchup, don't just look at the calories in the pie, you must include the calories in the sauce, so many people live in blissful denial because of this discrepancy.

To grow a portfolio, people are wrong to think they should choose to avoid negative gearing or include negative gearing in their plan.

The loan to value ratio (LVR), more specifically your level of debt versus the value of the property, and the cost of that debt and costs, versus income coming in from the property, will determine if the property is negatively geared.

Many properties can end up being positively geared, it just depends on what is able to be done with it, such as renovate or subdivide or borrow less, if possible, the lower the debt the more likely the rent versus debt and costs lead to the property being positively geared. For properties with less scope for development or manufacturing more value or yield, a debt reduction strategy can help.

Now: The question you should ask yourself is how best to move forward?

The answer is you must consider trying to maximise your outcome while also maximising your on-going borrowing capacity and equity/ cash position, while having an affordable balance with your current lifestyle having money for a rainy day and emergencies and have a degree of preparedness for rate rises and debt converting to principal and interest.

If you are focused too heavily on capital growth you will negatively impact on your borrowing capacity, as capital growth strategies often require a compromise on yield/cash flow, which mean you will earn less from the property while you own it (ignoring some potential benefits from renovating or developing). This is particularly in reference to blue chip suburbs. Regional suburbs do not fall under the common definition of 'blue chip'.

Outer suburbs from any capital city are not blue chip. Blue chip suburbs often require you to spend, as of the middle of 2022, closer to 2 million, or more, for a house. Yields (percentage of rental income against purchase price) are much lower than suburbs further out.

Yes, growth is more reliable, and yes you need money to make money, that is true, with more money, you can often make more money as there is more to leverage off and work for you. The risk is not the location itself necessarily with blue chip locations, it is affordability not just in buying but more importantly in holding the property long term.

To have a 1.6 mill+ loan on a 2-mill property is a large debt (1 egg in 1 basket), growth is more reliable, changes to your job, income, health etc. are out of your control far too often. If the property is vacant for some reason, the repayments still need to be made, excuses to the lender that the property was vacant and there will be a delay in the next repayment is useless information to a lender, why should they care very much.

The buyer of such properties ought to have put more thought into the purchase and bear full responsibility for their actions. If the owner failed to have a 3–6-month cash buffer for unforeseen circumstances, or they failed to ensure they could afford the debt if rates increased by 1-2%, well, they made their bed, they need to lay in it. However apathetic this may sound, it's what the reality is.

Of course, lenders have been helping mortgagors get through moments in time like being unable to make a repayment due to a life event, because a lender would rather, typically, not always, work with their customer, than sell them up.

During 2020 is an example where lenders helped people with repayment holidays through Covid. The mortgage was not reduced, it was increased, capitalizing the interest due onto the debt and therefore in most cases increasing the future repayments, given the loan term remained the same for a higher amount of debt to be paid off, but hey, that's to be expected.

Some people considered it wise to pay the amount of interest they didn't pay during the repayment holiday, because a smart person, who's job, health and life were unaffected by Covid and the repayment holiday may have been purely precautionary, would have banked their wages and saved the wages (not gone shopping, gambling etc) that would have ordinarily gone toward repayments, then pay the bank a lump sum to catch up, therefore avoiding the unpaid interest being added to their mortgage and in turn insuring their future repayments didn't increase due to this.

If you earn less on a property than what you could on another property, the holding cost is higher. It could affect you, your family, your budget, and the ability to enjoy life now. You could become trapped to your debt, forever forced to work just to afford the debt. This vicious cycle is best avoided.

In retirement, it is obvious you need income or a source of money. It is important to have some excellent cash flow producing properties, whilst it is as equally important to not have too much debt, thus avoiding the 'cost of the debt' mitigating the benefit of the potential positive cash flow nature of the properties.

Whether you are starting out or midway through your property journey, or nearer retirement, you continually need to assess your options of how geared (ratio of debt to value of assets) you wish to be.

Starting out on your journey may require you to borrow to a higher amount against the value of the property, the Loan to Value Ratio (LVR) as you may not have much saved or have not accumulated any capital growth in any assets. Later in life you hopefully would have built up some equity and/or saved some cash.

A higher price property could expose you to being out of your comfort zone and if the property is vacant, you have a larger debt to cover. If the price is lower and you spread any borrowing capacity over several properties, you can reduce this risk, but it would also limit the dollar figure of growth associated with the property.

For example: If a million-dollar property grows 10%, this equal $100k capital growth. If a $500k property grows 10% in value, this is $50k capital growth. Conversely, if there is an 80% debt against the million-dollar property i.e., $800k, and for some reason it is vacant, you have a super large debt to make repayments on.

If a $500k property has an 80% debt (i.e., $400k) and it happens to be vacant, you have a much more affordable debt or cost of debt to make repayments on.

In general, a lower priced property has better yield than a higher priced property. Having more properties around the $600-800k price could produce more rental yield (as a percentage against the value of the property, not in dollar terms) than the same number of properties valued around $1-2 million.

Comparison of a unit versus apartment versus a townhouse, versus a house.

You cannot always compare these as easily as you may like. A well-purchased unit may outperform an averagely purchased house. Conversely, you could have purchased a house in Doreen, Vic, in 2016 for roughly the same money as a 2-bed apartment in Preston, Vic. Preston has, by most people, always been regarded as a better suburb than Doreen, however, what do you get for the same money is the question. 4 beds, 2 bath, 2 car houses in Doreen have grown more in value than a 2 bed 1 bath 1 car apartment in Preston, even though Preston is recognised as a better suburb. A better suburb is typically based on its proximity to the city. So, for the same budget, you would have done better for what you could have purchased for the same money in a lesser-known suburb.

Always compare apples with apples. A house in Preston versus a house in Doreen would have been a different story, but every investor has a certain borrowing capacity, and it is what you do with that money that matters, not just 'what' or 'where' but both 'what' AND 'where' you buy is important.

After all your research, you can compare the performance of a suburb within your budget and the past growth of specific sized dwellings. Units, apartments and townhouses often offer better proximity to amenities and transport and are more affordable than a house in the same suburb. Units and townhouses provide higher yield, the owners corporation usually includes building insurance, whereas, normally with a house, you will pay this yourself. Note though, the owner's corporation fees, previously known as body corporate fees, can erode and fully mitigate the higher yield.

Some master planned housing estates have popped up and the houses in some of these estates do have owner's corporation costs as well. It is no longer just units, apartments and some townhouses that have owner's corporation costs.

In Victoria, less than 3 dwellings (townhouses) on a block of land won't normally have strata fees (owners corporation), though in Qld, will normally pay excruciating strata fees for just 2 dwellings on the block, quite the rort.

Specific parts of Qld have shown amazing capital growth the last 12 months, particularly the last quarter of 2021 and first half of 2022, however, there are so many parts of Qld not worth investing in, and the extortionate costs associated with insurance and council rates, very quickly erode the often-higher rents achievable there, therefore, recently, people are buying for growth rather than the previous overused misleading belief that Qld was good for capital growth, now this has become reality. Yield has usually been the driver for investment in Qld, alas, as mentioned, if you purchase a bog-standard property there, cash flow benefit is eroded by costs.

Units offer lower maintenance, come with more land than apartments, apartments offer little to no garden for the tenant to manage, and common ground is the responsibility of the owner's corporation, not the owner. Units, townhouses and apartments offer 'would be' investors a more affordable way into the property market.

Some people, in NSW for example, refer to units as villas. Some people confuse units and apartments. A unit is a free-standing dwelling, sometimes abutting one or two other dwellings, sometimes not, they do not have a common entrance for entry into them, they may of course have a common drive. Apartments have a common entrance; they are stacked above each other and will have stairs or a lift or both.

Townhouses are often a great compromise for a lower budget to buy in a better area, they are between a unit and a house.

They will not grow as much as a house in the same suburb, but they may be better than a unit in the same suburb, and better than an apartment in the same suburb.

Apartments have less land on title than a unit. A unit sits on its own bit of land, an apartment sits in a building with other apartments. Except for those on the ground floor, apartments do not sit on their own plot of land. They simply have a percentage allocation of the land the whole building sits on, a very watered-down value compared to a unit, townhouse or house.

Developers have ravaged the landscape and skyline in many locations; many suburbs are simply plagued with apartments. If you can, consider buying a unit, townhouse or house, in high-density suburbs especially. Some locations are more conducive to apartments, units and townhouses than houses.

Recently I assisted a first home buyer purchase a townhouse in a suburb known for its prevalence of houses, however, due to affordability, with all the benefits of amenities and infrastructure, a townhouse was better for the client, and it allowed her to avoid stamp duty as it was no higher than 600k.

We secured a loan of 98%, no lenders mortgage insurance (LMI), with the inclusion of the government scheme assisting single parents.

The client was also entitled to the first home buyer grant, given the townhouse was brand new, built, but never lived in. What a great outcome for a first home buyer.

Units and townhouses may have perhaps 120-300 sqm of land they sit on, with units being single story and townhouses double story (main difference).

The next diagram (overleaf) demonstrates the difference between buying an older house versus a new townhouse from a cash flow perspective, it is not to say it is better to purchase a townhouse, as the capital growth would be lower, however, for some people, cash flow is more important or budget more restrictive.

Both properties are assumed to be the same price in the same suburb just for demonstration purposes as to the differences in the properties beside price, based on an actual case study.

The house has more land, and the house (dwelling on the land) would not have as much value as the land it sits on, most of the value would be in the land, so the sale price may be roughly the same as a brand-new townhouse. A townhouse would have less land, but most of the value is in the dwelling.

You will see that even though buying a house will provide more capital growth in this realistic example, it will limit you as to the amount of wealth the investor *could afford* to create, as the cost of owning the portfolio could be prohibitive. Wealth creation would be more with the house normally but affording to own and hold the property long term is the important point, in order to have made that wealth.

If it was that easy, everyone would have purchased in Balwyn Victoria for example, or an equally renowned blue-chip suburb in elsewhere.

Purchasing a townhouse would likely provide less growth than a house in the same area but it may allow more properties to be purchased because there is more depreciation on the dwelling and the ability to claim depreciation on the fittings and fixtures if no one else has previously owned it.

More debt may be able to be afforded possibly leading to similar wealth to be created over time as more cash flow could allow more properties being purchased based on more borrowing capacity, greater ability to sleep at night knowing the debt is more affordable, more comfort than taking on more debt, buying another property, diversifying and perhaps closing the gap on the capital growth difference between the townhouse and the house by being more able to own another property.

Here is the crucial process of sourcing a good property

	ESTABLISHED HOUSE	NEW TOWNHOUSE
Price	600k	600k
Land Size	550sqm	290sqm
Capital Growth	8.50%	5.50%
Stamp Duty	30k	8k
Rent	$440	$460
Interest Rate	4.50%	4.50%
Interest repayment type	I/O	I/O
Rental expenses* including rates, agents commission, letting fee, landlord and/or building insurance, maintenance, bodycorporate	30%	24%
Depreciation on Building	0	yes
Depreciation on fittings and fixtures	0	yes
Income (wage) of investor	90k	90k
Tax saving year 1	4.9k	8.87k
Holding cost per week^	$148	$33

	ESTABLISHED HOUSE	NEW TOWNHOUSE
Number of properties owned in 10 years	1	4
Price of other purchases	0	550k x 3
In 10 years, the compounded value in the example is	1.357 million	4.9 million

Some points worth noting on this example are:

- Differences include no body corporate on the house, so building and contents insurance $1200. On the townhouse, there is body corporate of $1200, which does include building insurance. Landlord insurance $250. Maintenance for a new townhouse, say $500 a year at the start. Established property say $2,000 a year at the start.

- The cost of $33 per week to own one townhouse will make it considerably easier for an investor on a lower income to afford, and it is assumed it will make it easier to then buy more. In this example, I have used three more properties. Four properties at $33 a week costing around the same as just one established property.

- Let's assume the second property was purchased in year two, the third property in year five and the fourth property in year seven. The figures represent the combined compound growth of these four properties, versus just the one house.

- The investor could have 4.9 million versus 1.37 million. It is a big mistake to look at each property in isolation to the bigger picture. It is also a mistake to consider buying 4 townhouses rather than one house, if possible, it would be better for wealth creation to buy more houses, and buy established properties, not brand new. Brand new may help with cash flow, however, you are paying a premium price for the property. Wealth is in the land, not the dwelling. Wealth is paying a fair price, not by paying the premium price a developer charges. Therefore, this example is useful for people with lower income or that prefer the comfort of a property costing them less to hold it. Wealth creation would be better if 4 houses were purchased rather than 4 townhouses. The dilemma now seems obvious, that is finding a balance between building wealth and affording to build wealth.

Wealth creation is certainty still a reality with a new house and land package in the outer suburbs, and it will be cheaper to buy such a property than an established property closer to the city, however, buying an established property in the same suburb as a new one may be better for an investor, for an owner occupier, I agree that new is often nicer than old.

> **RULE:**
> *Always do the best you can with what you have, it is almost always better to invest wisely than not invest at all.*

> **RULE:**
> *Find a balance between wealth creation and affordability to suit individual circumstances.*

> **RULE:**
> *Always consider the value of the land as a component of the purchase price and value.*

Land size is less important than the value of the land for the size it is. In other words, 400sqm of land within 10km of the CBD of Melbourne is worth more than two acres of land in some suburbs 90km from the CBD, and worth more than 600sqm of land in a regional area, unless of course you're a farmer, in a growth corridor of a major city and a developer offers you millions for your land.

The gap is decreasing with the mass exodus of people leaving Victoria and large cities, due to several reasons, frustration with their respective Premiers, tired of lock downs, more space so if there are future lock downs they are not trapped and couped up in a smaller dwelling in the claustrophobic environment of a city.

When you hear houses perform better than units, be cautious as to where they are, and what you are comparing. For example, a house in Werribee, Vic, typically may not perform as well as a well purchased unit in Ivanhoe, for example.

Residential property falls into two broad types.

Type 1: Unwanted, to be avoided.

For purposes of comparison, let's rule out most of the less desirable stuff.

Whether you consider buying regionally, in outer suburbia of a metro location, or near the CBD of a capital city, there are many choices in the type of property that can be purchased, such as, studios, units, apartments, townhouses and houses.

Serviced apartments

Lenders will limit what you can borrow to as low as 60 percent of the value, which means putting in more of a deposit, leaving less money available for growing a portfolio. Far too often, the owner's corporation (body corporate fees) can be high and there can be an expectation to spend circa 15k every 5 years to update the furniture. The higher rental is often mitigated by the costs of ownership.

Often, the owners' corporation agreement prevents the owner from residing in the property, lenders do not like being dictated to by owners' corporations' covenants and restrictions.

Student accommodation

Limited LVR, like serviced apartments. Limited tenant appeal, resale appeal, and capital growth.

High-rise, high-density apartments

I call them coffins in the sky, often resembling shoe boxes, and often there is an oversupply of these, therefore tough competition with many other owners to find tenants, often forcing the owner to reduce rent. The same applies to future resale, at any one time there may be several up for sale, and sale price could be negatively impacted.

Most lenders will limit their lending to 70%, sometimes 80%, if situated in a high-density postcode, such as 3000, or 4000. Owners' corporation costs can be high, especially if the building has several lifts, a pool, gym etc.

Under 50sqm in size or Studio apartments

There are a few lenders that will allow below 40sqm, many requiring minimum 50sqm of living, excluding balcony, car park, or storage box. With Covid lock downs, people have realised how claustrophobic these truly are, leading to the lowest level of interest in these types of dwellings in recent times.

Off the plan apartments

There is a big risk the valuations will come in lower, at least on more than 50% of occasions, requiring the contribution of more capital.

Finance approval will usually expire within three to six months. So, think about it, if the property takes longer to be built, finance would have expired and unless you are able to extend your finance approval, or be approved again, you will LOSE your deposit.

Often rental guarantees are misleading as to their benefit, prices are often inflated, these schemes are generally misleading. Occasionally they are good, it just depends.

National Disability Insurance Scheme (NDIS), Defence housing

Most lenders won't touch these. NDIS can provide excellent income, however, the seriously significant modifications often included/required in these properties (lower vanity height, ramps, handrails, lower kitchen bench tops, lower toilets) leads to a limited resale market also, limited pool of potential buyers by default, demand aids capital growth, limited demand can negatively impact on capital growth. For cash flow they can be fantastic, so this is not necessarily definitely belonging on this list.

NRAS (National Rental Affordability Scheme)

These can be in good areas and can provide great tax incentives. Far too often though, developers and property marketing companies have bastardised this market (building them in great numbers, in poor locations).

Lenders typically will only use 80% of the 80% of market rent, thus, negatively impacting on borrowing capacity, lenders normally don't factor in the tax credits associated with them. So, these can be good, and don't necessary deserve to be on this list, depending on what and where it is, the consortium managing the tax credits and a raft of other considerations.

Display Home

Many lenders don't touch these, and if they do, its best the builder is not using it for a display home still. Rent guarantees are not palatable by lenders, as they are short term, and long-term loan affordability is ignored if borrowing capacity is based on a flash in the pan income. Besides, hundreds of people trapsing through the property is more a commercial use.

Resort style

Lenders don't like these, they have a limited resale and tenant market, often exorbitant owner's corporation fees and covenants, preventing the owner from residing in the property.

Locations and other features to avoid

- Properties on main or busy roads
- A dwelling above a shop
- High tension power lines within 50-100 metres (they have limited appeal, and are unsightly)
- Sloping blocks, especially for potential development
- Kit and portable homes
- Buying or financing a semi-completed property
- Vacant land (this is not considered investment, you cannot pitch a tent and call it home, no deductible interest benefits to assist with borrowing capacity)
- Flood zones

Mining towns

A prime example of one of the worst places to have invested in Australia is Moranbah, though Qld and WA are often associated with a great number of bad investment areas, once you start buying away from popular places like parts of Perth (though, even has been questionable in recent years, it is in its cycle though, it is still worth investing in certain parts, like anywhere), Brisbane, Sunshine Coast and Gold Coast.

Any one-horse town is a bad investment choice. A one-horse town is where there may only be one or two industries in the town. If one industry dies, the town will die. You need jobs to attract people to stay, you need multiple industries to absorb the hit from one industry dying.

Wrong type of dwelling for the area

It is always important to purchase a property that suits the widest demographic possible, the more demand for the type of property the more quickly its rented and the more easily and profitably its eventually sold.

For example, in the outer suburbs of major capital cities, a house may be more suitable than a one-bedroom apartment. Inner metro locations are more conducive to apartments and townhouses, though a 2-bed apartment is more popular than a 1 bed apartment, a townhouse even more so than an apartment. A unit, as distinct from an apartment (i.e., one of less than a dozen or two, single level, free standing) is often a better investment than an apartment in the same area where both may be prevalent.

I knew a property marketing spruiker in the past, who unconscionably promoted and sold 3 beds, 1 bath houses to unsuspecting investors, in suburbs where the overwhelming demand was for 4 beds, 2 bath houses. Be very careful in buying through property marketing companies. Some properties are good, and only through some of these companies.

Focus on areas that are sustainable, with good past capital growth, 'promising' future growth, and/ or good cash flow, in locations with several industries, good population growth and income growth. Purchase the most suitable type of dwelling.

It's not enough to buy in a good suburb, you need to purchase the right type of property in the better pockets of the suburb (a good example may be Hawthorn, if you purchased a 1 or 2 bed apartment 5 years ago, you would likely have done very poorly, compared to purchasing a house in the same suburb).

Don't fall for the trap of being too focused to buy under median price, you'll end up buying in the worst parts of the suburb (as these are typically cheaper and make up the bulk of the properties below median price. The better parts of the suburb will normally be above median and are more liveable for owner occupiers. There can be exceptions, such as the ripple effect of price growth, or, gentrification leading to price growth, and affordability can create demand.

Type 2: Pretty much the standard types of properties such as a unit, apartment, townhouse, villa.

Most investors purchase these standard types of properties to buy and hold. Houses can be purchased for many more strategies including renovation, flipping, subdividing, development.

Properties can tick the boxes of yield, and capital growth more so by, manufacturing growth and cash flow with subdivision and development.

As time progresses, the purchase price is assumed to go up, assuming you have sought advice, or undertaken adequate and supporting/useful research and purchased in a good area and an appropriate dwelling in that area, so the more spread out the acquisition phase of this plan the more you will probably pay for each property.

A property now, in a given suburb, will be more expensive in the same suburb in five years typically. Dilemma: buying more properties in a shorter time to keep the price lower versus buying them over a longer period, for comfort and affordability reasons, and paying more for them.

Any time a client shortens the acquisition phase and lengthens the holding phase, they're maximising the holding period to try and achieve better results.

Should You Buy a New or Older Investment Property?

The higher rent, likely less repairs and maintenance, higher desirability for a tenant, possibly lower stamp duty (not in Victoria), lower holding cost, more depreciation, greater affordability to grow a portfolio, and builder warranty, combined with any negative aspects of some new property, could still equal or be better than an established dwelling.

An established dwelling with lower rent, may be less desirable for tenants (depending on what it's like inside, and the cost to rent) and higher repairs and maintenance risk, higher stamp duty, higher holding cost, less to no depreciation, with no builder warranty, but better capital growth (depending on what you are comparing it to), is worth considering more than a brand new, not yet built property or a property being sold by a marketing company, it just all depends on your needs, wants and the property.

Valuations not stacking up with new property is a common risk, very very common. Claiming the depreciation is not the gilded lily many people think.

It simply makes the holding cost of the property more affordable until sale, as mentioned earlier, you will be severely stung when you sell, you will pay ALL the depreciation back to the Government.

Benefits of New Property

- If you wish to reduce risk of repairs and maintenance, then new is handier, this reason alone is a weak one though.
- Light and space are maximized is often an argument, but it depends on the builder.
- They usually offer more depreciation benefits; investors can use these tax benefits to assist with monthly cash flow.
- Stamp duty savings, depends on the State, Victoria is a big fat no.

Disadvantages of New Property

- You pay a premium compared to older properties in the same area.
- Too many similar properties being sold at the same time; depending where.

- Difficult to add value by renovating or extending.
- Some marketing company/developer/spruiker is making 30-50k in commissions which most of the time they do not disclose. If they do not disclose this, this, in my opinion is unethical, they should be ashamed.

New Property Valuations

Things that may not be considered in a valuation:

- Level of finish/quality, better quality means the construction contract price is higher.
- Lack of comparable sales in the location. Developer sales are not considered acceptable comparable sales.
- Values not understanding the product i.e., dual occupancy.
- GST; a few lenders deduct this from the sale price.

Refer to www.propertyinvestingmadesimple.com.au to understand more about house and land style contracts, and off the plan.

Benefits of Older Property

- More chance to negotiate.
- You can potentially add instant value through renovating, extending, subdividing and/or developing.
- Older properties are often situated on larger blocks, which usually drives property value upwards.
- Better if found in well-established suburbs, which can demonstrate consistent growth.

Disadvantages of Older Property – these are no excuse most of the time

- Lower rental rates.
- Higher maintenance costs.
- Lower depreciation.
- Higher holding costs.

4

Finance

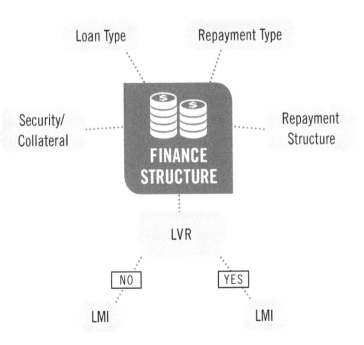

> **RULE:**
>
> *Avoid using a company that is vertically integrated, i.e., they have their own finance division, property division and even conveyancing division, there are too many horror stories to mention that have resulted from people using these types of organisations. There is quite simply a complete lack of accountability if everything is done in house.*

When considering buying any property, the most important thing you need to know is what you can afford to borrow.

Until you know this you cannot start looking for a property, unless you just want to waste your time looking at pretty pictures on online platforms, which is a bit masochistic as well if you end up not being able to buy anything you've looked at.

I recommend using a mortgage broker. There are so many reasons why you should not go straight to a bank. My recent book is a must read for you to understand this in much more detail: www.propertyfinancemadesimple.net.au.

Bank branches can place a great deal of pressure on their 'in house' loan writers, expecting them to cross sell insurance, financial planning services and other types of debt like credit cards and personal loans.

As recent events have demonstrated, even the biggest banks can be investigated for scandals, selling the wrong insurance products to the wrong people, and end up investigated by the regulatory authorities for alleged involvement in money laundering and corrupt activities.

> ### RULE:
> *When obtaining finance, do not go directly to a bank; use a good mortgage broker.*

When assessing what is best suited to your needs, you need to consider the loan type and features such as, for example, a redraw facility, an offset account, a fixed rate loan, length of time to fix the loan, variable rate loan, and whether you pay lenders mortgage insurance.

Every lender is different as are their borrowing capacity calculators. Your borrowing capacity may vary by tens and tens of thousands.

The cost of the mortgage, when doing your sums, should never be based just on current interest rates, but rather the potential future cost of debt, by factoring in a reasonable buffer. Look at 'repayment figure' not 'interest rate' to understand the cost to you as well, regarding fees, set up costs etc.

There are many cases where a lower rate can equal higher repayments, compared to a slightly higher rate equalling lower repayments, due to lower fees. The most important consideration beside cost is whether the loan gives you what you want, this is determined by policy, whether the policy of that lender ticks all your boxes. It is a minefield out there and can be quite frustrating doing it yourself.

Most people focus on the 'now', not the 'what if'. The modelling of holding costs – considering interest rates, lending criteria, income being earned, unexpected changes in personal circumstances – and being better prepared, is so important. Not factoring in the potential future cost of debt in conjunction with actual living expenses (which may differ to the standard expenses the lender will factor in), is the craziest thing you can do when applying for a mortgage.

Deciding when to fix or have your rate variable

Ultimately, it's a question of risk appetite. If a person has a low-risk appetite, perhaps fixed rates are important. It is not necessarily about making or saving money as much as it is about minimising short term future risk of repayments changing.

Variable rates used to be tied to the market but they're now at regular and on-going 'risk' at being changed as and when, and to what, the given lender feels in the mood for at the time, especially for interest only on investment and owner-occupied loans and principal and interest repayments on investment.

To hedge your bets, perhaps you may consider half fixed and half variable; it's a personal decision.

Fixing the rate can be a short-term risk reduction strategy. It provides piece of mind that for the selected period the interest rate won't change, and the repayment will stay the same. Bear in mind the lender has priced the fixed rate to the projected market, meaning you may likely pay more now for a fixed rate, and by the time variable rates catch up, the saving you may make for the remainder of the fixed rate term may have been considerably eroded by the additional cost of having the fixed rate for the period up until variable rates are higher. The banks have more resources than you or me – you cannot outsmart them. Anecdotally, over the last roughly 20 years it works out about the same.

Principal and Interest (P&I)

These loans have higher repayments than interest-only loans, as some of the repayment is going toward reducing the loan principal (debt amount) over the life of the loan. At the start of the usual 30-year loan term most of the repayment is interest, but over time, the principal component increases as a component of the repayment. You will note in the next diagram, the amount of interest saved on a principal and interest loan, is roughly $237,000.

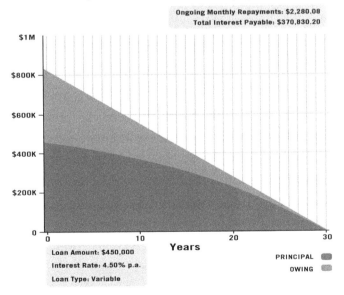

Principle & Interest Loan Repayments

Ongoing Monthly Repayments: $2,280.08
Total Interest Payable: $370,830.20

Loan Amount: $450,000
Interest Rate: 4.50% p.a.
Loan Type: Variable

PRINCIPAL
OWING

Interest-Only (I/O)

For a period, usually up to five years, the borrower only has to make interest repayments on the mortgage and does not need to pay back any of the money borrowed during this period. Investors have traditionally applied to the same lender or refinanced to a different lender to continue to only have 'interest only' repayments, thinking that they will worry about paying back the debt in 30 years' time, or certainty not in the next 10-20 years. This can be a big mistake. See the next example of the difference in interest you will pay over 30 years with an interest only loan versus a principal and interest loan, roughly $237,000 more interest will be paid from you to the lender.

Yes, the repayments per month go up but you are then not relying solely on the capital growth of the property to pay off the debt and provide wealth when you eventually sell the property.

Additionally, with principal and interest repayments you are reducing the debt and future exposure to that original debt. Eventually you may not even need to sell the property, you can simply live off the rental income from the property with no cost of debt against it. The more properties in this situation, the better.

Remember to focus on reducing the non-tax-deductible debt on your home as a priority. To break with tradition, this does not necessarily have to be done prior to reducing the debt against your investment properties. It all depends on your situation. Certainly, if you have paid off your home loan, you ought to consider reducing your investment loans.

Interest Only Loan Repayments

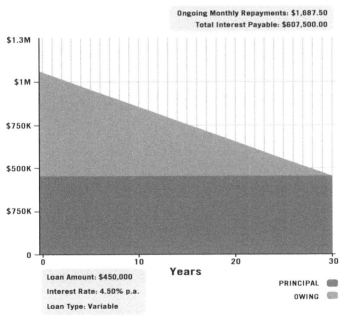

Ongoing Monthly Repayments: $1,687.50
Total Interest Payable: $607,500.00

Loan Amount: $450,000
Interest Rate: 4.50% p.a.
Loan Type: Variable

PRINCIPAL
OWING

RULE:

Over many years, whether you fix your rate or leave it as a variable interest rate, research has shown that you will break even and achieve nothing financially different either way.

5

Research and Locate

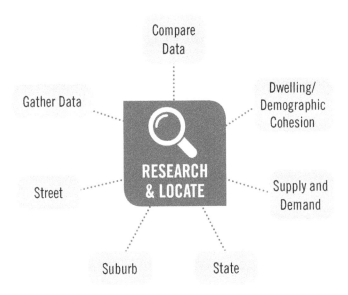

First let's consider the basics.

You have a plan, with the required number of properties in it and what each one looks like. You have a strategy; it could be buy and hold or renovate/developer and flip. It could be capital growth or cash flow or a balance of both from the same property.

Properties may include a house, townhouse, unit, apartment, villa, terrace, dual occupancy, land, and multiples of these depending on the strategy.

The strategies are broken down into two key aims or needs, growth and cash flow. These are needs that you must meet between now and your ultimate goal of a comfortable retirement. As discussed, budget, affordability and your tailored plan will influence the following choices.

- The State within Australia that you purchase each property in.
- Metro or regional

Then:

1. Metro 1: within 10km of the CBD
2. Metro 2: within 20km of the CBD
3. Metro 3: within 30km of the CBD
4. Fringe: 30km–40km of the CBD
5. Metro: satellite cities/growing hubs
6. Regional hubs

> **RULE:**
> *Avoid what many investors do. Many investors are drawn towards innuendo, media hype, and listening to friends, family, and backyard self-acclaimed experts, and worse, property marketing companies and real estate agents.*

The real issue, which inadvertently leads to failure, lies in not undertaking proper research.

There is no real rulebook out there, until now …

Here are some respectable and risk-reducing considerations that should make your job easier in finding an outperforming location. This also reinforces why it is important to seek objective advice.

Research must be based on facts and figures, and reliable information – unbiased information. This goes for information provided to the investor, and the information the investor is basing their own decision on, as well. Often property investors can fall into the trap of using their own emotion, beliefs, attitude, and experiences to base decisions on, such as where to buy and what to buy, and the inclusions in the property itself. What you or I personally prefer has no relevance when compared to what the area suggests is needed, in reference to the type of dwelling being more suitable to the demographic.

Check the position that State of Australia is in, in regard to the property cycle – property cycle refers to the period of time over which the price of a property changes by being influenced from demographic, economic and supply and demand changes in the area; each area may have its own cycle and be at different stages than another area – and whether it is at the bottom, middle, or top of the cycle. It is always a good time to buy, but not everywhere, at any given time.

The peak would be 12 o'clock on a clock (end of the boom), 6 o'clock would be the trough (bottom of the market). Between 12 o'clock and 3 o'clock is a correction, 3-5 must avoid, 5-9 is opportunity. It is difficult to know when the top or bottom is going to be. Between 11 and 12 o'clock you might want to exercise caution.

Looking at supply and demand in conjunction with population migration is one of the most important points, as is wage growth. An example of an area to avoid is Docklands in Melbourne, with the oversupply issues and extremely high vacancy rates. If, however, you look at population migration in isolation you may be led to believe it is a perfect area, hence why it is so important to review population with supply.

If people were not attracted to the area, the area would unlikely increase in value. The fundamental figures start with supply and demand, like any commodity. If there is no demand, then it has little true value.

The more important element of the location is its infrastructure. Some infrastructure is merely 'being discussed' by council, and other authorities, as to 'whether it will be planned'. Then it may end up 'being planned' and move forward to being a 'committed plan'. Once the infrastructure has commenced, you can be certain that it is in full swing, and it will have a tangible end result. The best solution here is to select a location where there are several existing industries. Be careful if you're acting on something that is only being discussed. It needs to be approved.

You must avoid one-industry towns, because if government contracts cease or spending there ceases and the population is very small, the town will probably die, capital values will drop, and vacancy rates will rocket up.

The economy of an area and surrounds, including the amenities there already (and in the pipeline), are important to know. In metropolitan locations, properties in suburbs with train stations tend to grow more than suburbs without stations. Hospitals, schools, other transport, and shops are important too.

The demographics, particularly for guiding you in making a more informed decision about the 'what' you should buy in the area, are very important for your budget, growth, rental, and any works needed on the property, and whether those renovations will improve the value. It also tells you the number of renters in an area. In some areas, units and townhouses are more popular and will have appeal to a greater percentage of the population. In other areas, duplexes or houses are better.

The number of renters versus owners will impact on the upkeep and future desirability of pockets within a suburb.

Vacancy rates (and not just the current rates, but how they are trending) will help you see if the area is becoming more popular or losing people. A simple snapshot will not demonstrate this, as it only captures a moment in time. When you look at shares you would normally look at trends, so do the same with property.

This methodology applies to the following points: Capital growth history, yields, days on the market, discounting and auction clearance rates, median house prices, population, supply and demand, vacancy rates, stock on market, income and employment growth is also very important.

Many people think that when a property has been on the market for two months nobody wants it (many people do not invest wisely though). I see opportunity. Maybe the vendor has been out of touch with reality of what the property is really worth. The agent normally has signed a three-month contract to sell it, both the vendor and agent may be more pliable and agreeable to a lower price. Look at the best streets; try to stay within a couple of blocks of these streets.

Comparable sales and timing of these is very handy and vital to your negotiations. You can compare what similar properties sold for within the previous six months, within three months is better (this is what valuers and financial institutions use) and use this as ammunition; it also provides you confidence in what the property may be worth. Sales within 1km is best, others in the same suburb may still be okay if a little further away. Comparing land size within 10% or less variance and compare the same number of bedrooms and bathrooms – there is software that will do all this for you.

If new (not yet built): Just focusing on fittings and fixtures included in the property, quality, uniqueness is good but be aware of what other properties in the estate include.

In some large estates, schools, hospitals, shopping centres, and a train station may improve your property value in the future. Trains and access to transport are big factors in the investment being viable.

There is software out there, which allows you to drill down in a suburb and overlay your own preferences to find an ideal location within a suburb.

Figures suggest choosing the street wisely can deliver much more capital growth than the rest of the suburb, rather than just haphazardly buying in a suburb, and it is a low percentage of a suburb where ideal streets lie. You may wish to understand which streets have less public housing and streets where people earn more than other streets. Rent and yield is higher on some streets, and you can avoid streets with too many units or apartments and understand which streets have too high a percentage of tenants versus owner occupiers.

Of course, a good buyer's agent will have access to research programs. Leveraging off a buyer's agent and their access to data, experience and knowledge in combining all the data, can save you thousands in annual subscriptions for the same outcome, not to mention hundreds of thousands in buying the right versus wrong property and saving money when buying.

Even then, doing it on your own is fraught with danger, without leveraging off the experience and knowledge of a buyer's agent. I charge a fixed fee. Some buyer's agents charge a percentage, the problem I have with a percentage is that if the buyer's agent isn't good at negotiating, they make more money. Additionally, the buyer's agent is more incentive to convince the buyer to spend more.

The next diagram shows the flow of steps that should be followed when undertaking research. This is an unemotional process, in order to maximise results.

Here is the crucial process of sourcing a good property

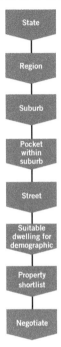

Median House Price

Median price can often be misleading and unreliable. Half the properties in a suburb are under the median price and half are over. Sometimes buyers think if they can buy under median they're doing well. Often the contrary is the case. It is not enough just to buy in a good suburb, although this is 75-80% of the work done, but it is important to buy in a good street in the suburb. The best streets in a suburb outperform the average and certainly outperform the worst streets. This then means you will be paying over the median price, which makes sense if you want to buy in the better part, the better part is going to be more desirable, more demand, and generally higher prices.

Of course, it is worth mentioning that if you purchase closer to median, on a better street or pocket of the suburb you are making money from day one.

Be very careful also of a false median. When new stock in an area comes onto the market or land has been carved up and two or three townhouses built on it, this can lead to sales of property in the area with prices way above the median. The sales prices can lead novice buyers to believe there has been significant capital growth in the area, when in fact prices may not have even risen. What could have happened is one of many things. For example:

- A newer property has sold for more than an older property.
- Larger parcels of land, or development sites may have been sold.
- Of course, don't rely too heavily on the median price for a suburb for one more very important reason; the suburb is comprised of different sized dwellings.

Size can be:

- Number of bedrooms
- Size of each bedroom
- Number of living areas
- Number of bathrooms
- Size of land
- Garage versus carport
- Quality of inclusions is another consideration.

At a bare minimum, only ever use the median price of the size dwelling you are trying to buy, as a starting point, never the median for the suburb. Compare apples with apples in other words.

So, look at three-bedroom house and four-bedroom house medians separately, for example. This provides a more accurate guide as to what you would expect to pay for the same size dwelling. Accompanied by an online valuation containing comparable sales, this can be used to make a more informed decision as to what to offer at auction or what to pay during negotiations. It also allows you to compare the capital growth and yield based on a specific number of bedrooms to see which is more popular in the suburb, besides looking at the demographics of the area.

At auction, be prepared to walk away once the bidding exceeds your pre-approved loan figure combined with available savings (yes you have been smart enough to seek a pre-approval), or the bidding exceeds what the property is realistically worth. Your finance approval may be for more, but the valuation must stack up.

There is no point spending too much above what it may be worth, because, if the valuation your lender does comes in lower than what you paid, you must find the money for the shortfall, or increase your loan, which may mean increasing your LVR (loan to value ratio, which may then cost you LMI (lenders mortgage insurance). It also erodes your spare capital that could have been used for a rainy day or a deposit on another property.

The adage, the property is worth what someone is prepared to pay matters not, what matters is the valuation, not what you paid for it, not what you think it's worth.

The more popular the dwelling size and type, the easier it may rent, as there's more demand – ensuring you understand what the supply is in comparison to the demand of course.

Commercial Property

In Australia more than 4.7 million people are employed by over two million small to medium enterprises. Source (ABS). The industry is growing rapidly and exceeds 400 billion as of around the middle of 2022.

The biggest difference with this market and the residential market is the fact that more macro and Government policy conditions affect the commercial space. Economic as distinct from market conditions can vary across commercial property grades and regions.

Commercial property is riskier when it comes to vacancy. More macro level classifications apply to commercial property, more so than residential. Entire sectors can be affected at any one time in an entire region, rather than being more centric to a particular suburb. Tourist accommodation, retail property, office and industrial can all suffer in an entire region.

With Covid, I would not like to own office space in Melbourne CBD or anywhere for that matter, as the risk is great that employers may not wish to return to the premises, or they may want to downsize, realizing that employees can be trusted to work from home and productivity can be maintained, whereas previously employers were incredulous about this in the past.

The problem with commercial property is its inherent lack of long-term, stable growth – just like the stock market, which is directly linked to the corporate world.

Many experts say that there is a high percentage of business failure in the first two years. Dunn & Bradstreet research shows that more than 80% of business failures are related to cash flow (rather than sales pressures). Vacancy rates can be high which soon offset the previously accompanying higher yields, so yields now are no longer taken for granted as being at 8%, they can be around 5-6% quite often.

Commercial property may include a business, shop, retail, resort-style offices, factories, farms, multi-unit developments, warehouses, industrial units, mixed residential and commercial use, and income-producing properties. The list goes on.

The values of the properties concerned are based on the rental returns. Often the tenant pays all the outgoings (i.e., insurance, rates, and fit out). This is a different market and requires different knowledge and due diligence.

Strata offices were popular before Covid as people could rent them close to where they live, and it allowed them to escape the distractions and interruptions at home and expand their business at the same time. (Strata title refers to a situation where the individual/entity owns part of the property such as the dwelling, i.e., townhouse, unit or office, but they share ownership of the rest of the property such as some or all of the land, driveways, gardens, foyers, corridors in apartment buildings etc.

Normally more than two dwellings that share a drive or common land require a body corporate/ owners corporation to be established to insure the land and manage the responsibility of the shared areas. Caravan parks, resorts, retirement villages are more obvious examples of this.)

Constructing more than three dwellings on one title would normally require a commercial loan, however there is a lender that will lend up to ten on one title.

For your own free copy of my own personal comprehensive research checklist, please go to my website:

www.australianpropertyadvisorygroup.com.au/resources.

This checklist covers most things that should be considered when researching, there are instructions on the checklist of how best to use it.

RULE:

If you follow this process, you will dramatically enhance your ability to time the market better, take more advantage of out-performing potential, reduce the risk, and create balance between the effect on your lifestyle – and betterment your future.

6

Purchase

Now you have found a property, or your buyer's agent has found a property or short list of properties for you that suit your plan and property strategy, or PPR needs.

They have been well researched, finance is pre-approved, you have decided on a conveyancer to use, and you have a property inspector in mind.

You have spoken to your accountant to advise you if you should purchase the property in your own name or in the name of another entity, such as a company or a trust. Upon deciding which property, you want to purchase, you either attend the auction if there is one, or you start negotiating.

Auction

If the property is going to auction, it is important to consider a few important things.

Are you confident to bid on your own, or do you require a buyer's agent to bid for you? There are many games that are played at auctions, and you need to understand the rules of the game.

You need to decide on the maximum price you're prepared to bid and be prepared to walk away.

If you win at auction you need to have understood whether it is 5% or 10% you pay on the day by internet transfer, evidencing receipt of payment to the agent or bank cheque. You cannot change your mind. There is no cooling off period.

What if you pay too much for the property? I have seen situations where someone is happy with the price they paid, and they attempt to convince the lender of that, but instead of the valuation coming in at contract price it comes back $50k or even a $150k under. A $750k property being valued at $580k is an example of what I have seen. The likelihood of this happening is greater if you have not used a good buyer's agent, or you have purchased from a property marketing company spruiker (alias-your potential enemy).

If it was a new (not yet built) property then it would not be an auction, but the same risk of paying too much applies. I touched on this earlier but it's so important to reiterate, people often say the property is worth what someone is prepared to pay; normally the real estate agent says this as a flippant and quite ignorant throwaway line. You won't be so compliant with this way of thinking if you lose your 5-10% deposit because you cannot settle on the property.

What if the property has some major defects or many smaller but expensive issues you need to resolve upon purchasing it?

So, what can you do to try and reduce some of the risk?

You can pay for a property inspection to be done prior to auction, understanding of course, that you risk having wasted $380-$500, if you are unsuccessful at auction. A further $200-$300 could be wasted if a pest inspection was also done. What a great insurance policy in a way, it at least would provide more comfort in bidding at auction; it is a small price to pay to help avoid making perhaps a several hundred-thousand-dollar mistake.

You just cannot change the fact that you can't have a 'subject to finance clause' in the contract.

You could also try buying the property before auction. Some vendors will accept an offer, some want the offer to be a crazy offer, and others may simply accept a reasonable offer to avoid the risk of the property not selling at auction. If the vendor does accept an offer from you, you could negotiate to have the clauses inserted in the contract, however, this is not as appealing to the vendor when the buyer says I will buy it but for this and this and that, the vendor would like to want to impose auction conditions on the offer.

> ## RULE:
> *You cannot have a 'subject to finance' clause or 'subject to property and pest inspection' clause in the contract under auction conditions, you are not protected.*

Private treaty

With a private treaty, i.e., when a property is not going to auction, you can insert the clauses in the contract, subject to negotiations. Be wary of dodgy real-estate agents. One example is a property in Frankston, Victoria. The agent was willing to accept a finance clause but not a property inspection clause in the contract. This has problems written all over it and it would more than likely suggest that the agent knows there is a problem and lacks the integrity to tell you. In this case we walked away and later discovered there were in fact serious issues with the property. If you think you can always trust the sales agent, think again. There are some excellent ones of course, they are harder to find.

When there is a private treaty, different agents have different ways of handling the process.

> **RULE:**
>
> *Remember, they do not represent you the buyer, they cannot and will not represent you and your interests when they have been hired and will be paid by the vendor.*

In March 1999, the office of fair-trading released a video of the president of the REIQ stating, *'We have a legal, moral and fiduciary duty to promote and protect the interests of the vendor and have no interest in the purchaser.'*

There are several approaches the can agents take, and you need to ascertain which approach is the one you must follow.

- You submit a tender, putting your best foot forward and the agent presents all offers to the vendor. No second chance, this does not provide you the ability to negotiate, and you risk offering more than you may have needed to, or too little.
- You can negotiate with some back and forth until either you walk away because the vendor still wants more, or you agree on a price. This process

can be via email if in NSW, leading to an offer being submitted on a signed contract and presented to the vendor. If the agent asks you if you're willing to fill in a contract it suggests you are close, but not in Victoria. In Victoria, many agents will not want to waste their time with you until you submit any offer on a signed contract. In my book 'The 100k Property Plan; how to earn $100,000 per year from property', I will go into depth on differences between different states of Australia. Each state is different.

- Once you sign the contract in a private treaty situation it is normal to have seven days for property and pest inspection to be carried out, and 14 days for finance to be fully approved (in Victoria and NSW). In Victoria, you may have 30, 60 or 90 days agreed settlement period, sometimes 120 days. You could even negotiate 12 months, with access to the property prior, for your personal enjoyment. In NSW, it is 42 days. Again, other states will be covered in my next book.

7

Team

The importance of having a team around you cannot be overstated. No one has enough knowledge to wear every hat needed in a property purchase situation.

It is naïve for anyone to think they can do it all themselves. I will list the team in order of when you need them; some will naturally overlap, as it is not a perfect sequence.

RULE:

Use a good conveyancer/lawyer, one that will help you fill in the contract. A lawyer is often better as they can provide legal advice. A conveyancer, unless they are a lawyer, is limited in the advice they can provide. Conveyancer do not usually provide advice on the build contract if you are purchasing a house and land package, be careful.

1. Accountant

Make sure yours has initiative. Even more importantly, ensure that they specialise in investment property, or at least have adequate knowledge.

Benefits of an accountant are as follows:

- Determination of whether you buy in a trust name, company name or your own name.
- If in your own name, determination of the percentage of ownership split between all purchasers. Given the higher income earner will normally pay more tax, if you have someone not earning an income with a high percentage of ownership on title you could be paying unnecessary tax/unnecessarily losing what your entitlements may be for tax deductions.
- Help avoid purchasing too many negatively geared properties, as there could be no tax advantages in holding more than one or two negatively geared properties, as it could place the income below the tax-free threshold and result in a negative outcome.
- Correctly determine how any costs

for renovations be apportioned. Many people make the mistake of incorrectly claiming costs in their first tax return rather than the costs being apportioned as capital costs.

- A good accountant can ensure you don't miss out on claimable items for extra tax deductions.
- The accountant will help you look after your investment property, which is best done from day one, by minimising holding costs and helping ensure the property is more affordable.
- They help you plan your money more effectively in order to have a balance with your property ownership and any changing interest rates and the effect of the interest rate on the property. I've seen people buy in a company, but not realise there are absolutely no capital gains tax concessions. At least in their personal name they are entitled to a 50% tax concession on capital gains tax, if they own the property for more than 12 months.

Many people do not realise that by being entitled to claim depreciation on the property, they will end up paying more capital gains tax when they sell.

A quality property is not just about it doubling in value but it's also about not having a property that is costing you an arm and a leg. Accountants can assist you with preparing a profit and loss schedule, and a PAYG withholding variation (if applicable).

Do not use an accountant that receives kickbacks from referring you to someone selling properties – that accountant is no better that the dastardly spruiker.

2. Broker

A broker saves you time.

They compare banks' borrowing capacity calculators, to determine which will lend you the most and will offer you the most favourable interest rate and lowest fees and find a balance between the two.

Fees and rates can be compared online easily enough but borrowing capacity calculators cannot be compared as easily, so why waste your time doing this when a broker will do it for free.

A bank employee lacks the knowledge, diversity, depth of experience and range of products and solutions to add any real value to you in building a property portfolio.

A broker will package up the deal (ensure all required supporting documents are in order and attached), track its progress, and do all the leg work for you.

Avoid you incurring unwanted credit enquiries on your credit file.

What more would you want than someone doing all the legwork to review your current mortgage rate, find who will lend you the most money and give you the cheapest rate and fees and all for free.

3. Buyer's Agent and Property Advisor

A buyer's agent takes all the legwork out of finding a property. You need a buyer's agent specialising in helping find the type of property you require. This involves a different set of criteria to find the best property for you to invest in, rather than finding a property to live in.

As buyer's agents, we often meet people who unfortunately have trusted a real estate agent when buying an established property, or they have trusted a property marketing company when buying a new (not yet built) off the plan or house and land style property.

> **RULE:**
> *Buyer's agents represent the buyer. Real estate agents and property marketing companies represent the seller. DO NOT trust a real estate agent when buying an established property, if they say they will represent you, or a property marketing company when buying a new or established property, they sell off stock lists, use a buyer's agent to sift the wheat from the chaff.*

Research and due diligence are the most important things to undertake when buying any property, especially an investment property. Knowing which areas to buy in for capital growth or for cash flow around Australia.

Use a buyer's agent not limited to one state or one property type or strategy is important for all investors. It's important to have a balanced approach to capital growth and cash flow, reducing the likelihood of running out of equity for your next purchase or borrowing capacity with a bank. This goes for your PPR also.

When considering investing, so often people don't appreciate the time it takes to find the right property. They end up going around in circles, trying to sift through the seemingly limitless choices available, whilst actually not really understanding or appreciating there are very few properties that are considered investment grade properties.

Often you will end up going to many open house inspections, then perhaps an auction, or negotiation, only then to miss out, and do it all again, spending hours on an online portal.

People need to understand what street the property is on, what it's near to, aspect, size, layout, yield, tenant demand, supply and demand, covenants on the property. They should then have a property inspection that could highlight potential issues which could lead you to pull out of the contract and start the process all over again.

You need to consider the settlement period, terms of agreement and clauses as well. A buyer's agent can negotiate for you or bid at auction for you, which could save you the same if not more than the buyer's agent fee, compared to negotiating yourself.

Leverage off invaluable knowledge and experience, identifying the next potential investment grade location and property.

Access to properties that you may have never known about.

> ## RULE:
> *Whether established property, new, house, townhouse, unit, cash flow, capital growth, inner city, regional, interstate, buy and hold or develop or flip, use a buyer's agent.*

4. Conveyancer

Conveyancing tends to be an afterthought when buying property, however buyers can reduce the risk of their buying decision by consulting a conveyancer or solicitor before they sign a contract. They provide a practical approach to the buying process by not only alerting the buyer to potential traps and risks in the buying process but also in the undertaking of more effective due diligence when having found a property.

You must get your conveyancer to read over the contract before you sign it, and they must be licensed in the state in which the property is in, most are only licensed in one state.

They will ensure your rights are as protected as possible, such as having a subject to property and pest inspection, and a subject to finance clause.

With the property inspection clause, it is often written such as 'subject to no major structural defects' Seek advice to include the following, 'subject to the buyer's satisfaction', although this could be construed as too vague for the vendor. It just depends if the sales agent picks up on it, often I have had it sail through.

You may consider not dating the contract when signing. This can buy more time between when you sign it and when the vendor signs the contract, as usually the clauses commence from the date of contract. This is often better if it is a later date than the day the buyer signs the contract.

Try to insert a clause in the contract allowing access to the property up to 2-3 weeks prior to settlement for tenants to be shown through by the property manager you have engaged, provided the property is vacant. I would always recommend taking vacant possession.

The laws have changed recently in favour of a tenant. If you wish to do work to the property, if you have some concern with the tenant, and most definitely, if they are currently paying too little rent compared to market rent, ensure they are booted out prior to you taking possession. Booted out in the legal sense of course, that's not your problem though, it is the vendors, if a clause is inserted "subject to vacant possession".

With this latter point, I have purchased properties for a client which at the time of making an offer did house a tenant that was paying too little, the seller hadn't increased the rent in line with market rent.

If you take on the property with the tenant, they could likely take you to VCAT or the equivalent if you increase the rent to market rent, if the jump from what they are paying to what the market rent is, is too great. Easier to ensure the seller gets them out. Your settlement period will have to consider this.

For example, 60 days' notice, and time for the notice to be emailed or mailed, perhaps another 10 days may be appropriate, discuss with your conveyancer.

If the tenant is paying market rent and has been there for a while, you still don't know them, the vendor could lie and say they are great tenants.

Some tenants psychologically treat the property as their own, and this is good if they are neat and tidy and respectful people, bad if they have an attitude, are reluctant to allow open for inspections to have occurred during the sale process and/or live like pigs.

Other important reasons to use them include, but not limited to:

- Timely settlement to avoid penalties charged by the vendor.
- Any problems with p/work, title, contract, documents etc., are more likely to be addressed
- appropriately and in a timely fashion.
- Determination of entitlements, any adjustments for costs, such as rates, water etc., so no liability travels with the property.
- Assistance with the completion of forms.
- Communication between the lender/broker, and the vendor and conveyance firm representing the vendor.
- Titles registered correctly, in the correct ownership structure and correct ownership percentages.
- Determination and advice on any negative or limiting factors or factors the buyer should be aware of such as environmental limitations, covenants, easements, boundaries, caveats.

5. Property inspector

Arrange property and pest inspection once vendors have signed contract. Their fee may be around $400-$600.

Property Inspections- for both PPR and investment

This is necessary for new and established. Normally you have seven days from signing a purchase contract for a property and pest inspection to be carried out, but only if you inserted this clause in the purchase contract.

> **RULE:**
> *An independent building inspection is not only the smart thing to do, but also vitally important.*

An agent's 30 minute 'open for inspection' is not enough time for prospective purchasers to inspect the most important areas of a home, the subfloor, roof space and roof.

The subfloor may reveal numerous issues in a home that unless revealed prior to a purchase may cost a lot of money:

- Dead animals
- Mould on the ground
- Damp ground
- Water ponding
- Rotting timber stumps
- Concrete stumps reduced in size from concrete cancer
- Ducted heating ducts disconnected
- Subfloor timbers cut to accommodate bathroom wastes
- Lack of subfloor ventilation
- Asbestos
- Leaking showers causing mould or rot to timber and flooring
- Owners building rubbish and or belongings
- Termites.

And worst of all:

- No access point to inspect.

The roof space may also reveal numerous issues:

- Lack of ceiling insulation or insulation is aged and ineffective
- Old unused gravity feed hot water systems
- Old asbestos heater flues
- Vermin or signs of mice, rats, possums, birds
- Cracked roof tiles
- Owner's belongings and/or rubbish.

The roof and gutter:

- Blocked gutters
- Cracked roof tiles
- Cracked roof tile bedding mortar
- Weathered timbers, gables and fascia's
- Leaking flashings
- Owners' belongings, e.g., balls in gutters.

The report will identify whether any defects are a major or minor, and whether in fact they pose a safety issue and will be a handy reference if you do purchase the property; especially if future maintenance is required.

All new homes have a seven-year warranty period; however, the warranty for some components of new homes diminishes over time. A report can identify which items are still covered at any time during the subsequent seven-year period.

Do not blindly rely on this warranty though. All new constructions require a building surveyor to be engaged by the builder to provide inspections on up to three of the five build stages, normally, slab, frame and final stage.

The inspections can be limited with less regard for quality of work and owner's specifications. Often, they miss a number of things that are done that may not be to standard or code, such as plumbing and waterproofing, insulation not to requirements, and many other serious shortcomings.

Ensure you insert in your contract that a property inspector working for you, not the builder, inspects all work being undertaken.

Don't let presentation of a property distract you from looking for underlying defects.

Some defects may be of a minor nature but if left unattended could result in costly and time-consuming repairs in the future.

> **RULE:**
>
> *Property inspections are necessary for every property; you cannot just blindly trust the quality of the builder or their finished product.*

Pest inspection is also advisable for the following reasons:

- To identify if there are any pests present, in particular, termites.
- If conditions are the sort of environment that pests would like.
- Pest inspections may not be necessary for brand new properties.

> **RULE:**
>
> *Never blindly trust a builder, you must verify his work. Never trust a real estate agent or vendor, you must verify the state of the dwelling with an established property as much as a new property.*

6. Rental manager- for investment properties

Eight weeks out from handover of new property, or four weeks from settlement of an established property, start discussions with a rental manager. You could negotiate to have early access to an established property to allow the rental manager to show people around if there isn't already a tenant in there.

Whilst you may think the vendor would not like this, not every sale and purchase is perfect for both sides there is always compromise, this may be a compromise a vendor will accept, especially in a buyer's market.

It may be easier to engage the firm that the sales agent works for as they still have the keys, and they may already know the property quite well. They may not be your preferred choice but let's be pragmatic here.

Use them until settlement then ditch them after settlement and hand the reins over to your preferred rental manager.

Business is business, so if you think someone else will do a better job then go for it. You owe no loyalty to the sales firm; they represent the seller. Remember, they are the ones who have negotiated against you for you to pay more.

When choosing a rental agent, always look for:

- A well-established company with a good and well established or well experienced rental management team.
- Ensure the commission paid is well spent. This is generally 6- 8% plus GST for their management fee to collect rent and one to two weeks' rent for leasing. If you have two or three properties with one agent, you may be able to negotiate down to 5% plus GST. Always avoid companies that only have one property manager, it is incredibly frustrating when you cannot get hold of them, and they always seem to be out of the office, and if they are off for the day, there is no solution for you. This is no way to run a business, and you should not have to deal with such a firm.

7. Quantity surveyor for investment properties

Investors should always, always obtain a depreciation schedule. This is required for taxation purposes if you wish to try and save some tax.

This should be obtained as soon as possible, certainly prior to you submitting your next tax return after the purchase.

A quantity surveyor places a depreciable value on the building. It of course excludes the land value component of the purchase price, and they place a value on the fittings and fixtures in the dwelling. You will need to provide them the purchase price and construction price (if applicable).

Of course, you can no longer claim depreciation on fittings and fixtures on an established property, nor on a dwelling built prior to September 1987.

8. Building and landlord insurance options

Building and landlord insurance options should commence at least by the day before or day of handover. Generally, it may be advisable to insure the property the day you sign the contract. Imagine if you purchased a property in Qld, and it was the day after signing, and there was a flood, and the vendor wasn't insured. Almost all insurers wont knowingly insure for flood damage in a flood plain, having spoken to ten of them in 2022, only one would insure for flood in a flood plain, cost of the insurance premiums for this are a different matter.

Your bank may require the certificate of currency be provided prior to handover/settlement and would normally have to be at a value determined by the replaceable value figure provided by the valuer.

The cost of landlord insurance can range from $280 per annum upwards and perhaps closer to $1000 for building insurance; more in Qld given the regular floods they seem to receive; everything, from a property cost perspective is more in Qld.

Be very careful to look at council flood plain maps. Once council in Southeast Qld informed me, in May 2022, they were reviewing their flood plains and expanding them based on a different formula.

Choose wisely between landlord insurance providers to ensure you are receiving adequate protection. Bear in mind that if the property does have owner's corporation fees associated with it, this would typically include in the premium the building insurance cover, not landlord insurance cover. Consider obtaining common ground insurance if buying any property, which does share common ground.

8

The Great
Australian Dream Mindset

'Nothing comes from doing nothing.'
– William Shakespeare

I have a quick question for you to ponder.

It's the most important question you could ever ask yourself.

If we were connecting two, five or ten years from today, and you were looking back over those years to today, **what would need to happen for you to feel really happy with your life?**

Take a moment to really consider that question.

Imagine it's two years in the future and you're looking back to today:

- **What** progress would you like to have made for you to feel really happy with your life?
- **What** would need to have happened? I mean, for you to be *really* happy.
- **What** would need to have happened in your life financially?
- **What** amount of money would you like to have invested?
- **What** would your income be?
- **What** about your health and appearance?
- **Would** you like to be slimmer? Fitter?

And let us not forget your relationships – including your relationship with yourself.

Would you like to have unconditional love and self-acceptance for yourself and everything you are?

You can really get into the 'picture' of your ideal future. You can:

- *See it.*
- *Smell it.*
- *Touch it.*

Be swept away by it. Allow it to fill your consciousness.

It's a **great feeling** *'trying on'* your **new** life, isn't it?

Do you know why?

Because your **new** life is available to you **as soon as you start releasing all of your unconscious limitations** – doubts, fear, worry, struggle, resistance, etc. – that stand in the way of 'where' you are and 'where' you want to be.

Now, image you now have your first home or are now retired, you are very happy, and you have your family around you. If it is retirement as a goal you have, you have more than $5million in assets and a passive income of over $8000 per month? Your house is paid off; your car is paid off; some or your investment properties are paid off; you have $20,000 cash in an account to use; you are happy and have a smile on your face.

You are on a cruise; relaxing and enjoying it with your wife, your family, and friends. You provided this opportunity by the fruit of your labour, your foresight, and your investments. Isn't it a picture you can see yourself in it?

All you have to do is release your unconscious limiting beliefs. I know you can certainly do it.

What is Happiness?

Happiness means different things to different people. I often ask someone what is happiness for him or her? They need to create happiness in their lives, and often they stop, think and don't know the answer. The big question is: how can we pursue happiness when we are not even sure what it is? So, what is it that we want to attract, what do we want to be, and what do we want to do with our life? Let's look at some qualities that can bring aspects of happiness into our life.

Most people that have productive lives and are filled with happiness have a sense of optimism despite the many failures in their life. Why is that so?

This is because these people tend to treat failure as a way of learning or changing their perspective and are able to handle the same issue in a different way or to be able to move on. The learning they experienced results in an attitude of gratitude, appreciation, and value for what they already have. These people have an optimistic attitude and find their happiness by looking at the positives – they are grateful for the learning. This is in contrast with those who, instead of learning, are continually complaining about what they do not have, and often talk about their past. Past is history, and that's one thing you don't want to dwell on if you are to move forward.

Many a times we find that we remember the past in some distorted ways and we long and dream for situations that never were; so instead of creating our happiness in the present and in the future we turn towards a misconception of what life may have been like and idolize it into something that it never was or could have been.

To make matters worse, we can dwell on the issue by holding onto this image that we built in our heads and live in that myth. In pursuit of happiness, we need to release the past. This may not be easy for some people, and it may not happen in a day. The good news is that it is possible to release the past and have a clear vision of your future and move on.

We are all human and we need good friends, loving family, and supportive friends and colleagues to bring happiness to those moments when we have fallen into a slump, and to share our lives in good times as well. It is vital to have people in our lives that care, and it takes energy and effort to keep those relationships in working order.

Often sadness creeps into our lives when we start to compare our relationships with others and start to think that our relationships are not as good and begin to feel uneasy and inferior. However, it is important to remember that no two relationships are alike. Whether it's a friendship or a marriage, your relationship with each person needs to grow naturally, and caringly. This will flourish and benefit both of you and bring the happiness you desire.

We all need to be aware that when we have good relationships, we can have happiness. Relationships are important; no one can exist on their own, as we need fuel to keep us alive. If we do not nurture and look after these relationships, they will die. Perhaps many people are fooling themselves when they claim and believe that they are happy living their lives in isolation. They often call it their 'world', in their own heads and space: no one to worry about, no one to fight with, and no one to bother them. And the question is: how long can they be happy on their own? Research and studies show loneliness increases the mortality rate. And not many people will admit to it, but they are lonely because they believe they are too busy to worry about being lonely. Are they really being honest with themselves, or are they just fooling themselves?

There *is* a recipe for happiness and often we believe happiness will come from external situations, like our material wealth, and relationships. The truth is that our relationships with others and our relationship with ourselves are what bring a true contentment and happiness – one that does not exist in the materialistic wealth world. This is encouraging and empowering because when we know this, we have control of our own future and how we nurture others and ourselves.

There is no room for making excuses as to why we cannot move on and put all kinds of limitations on ourselves. We now have an ability to move on so that we can no longer become stuck and sabotage our lives. It is impossible to pursue happiness and move forward, or be able to grab any opportunities, when one is living a life of excuses and self-sabotage.

Whenever opportunities are offered to them, they have many reasons why they cannot do it. Or they make excuses that it was some other person's fault that they missed the opportunity.

If people continue to stay in that mindset, it is very difficult for them to achieve their goal in life or do what they really want to do.

If this applies to you, I need to tell you that you can now leave the negative – self sabotage mindset, bad attitudes, and negative beliefs behind and you can transform your life.

You can create a more positive outlook and actually build new neurological pathways in your brain. And this means you can move forward physically, mentally, and spiritually and achieve what you really want (and always wanted) to do.

The following case study is of Pearl Yeo; a dear friend and a valuable contributor to this book. Pearl's story is told in her own words.

Case Study

'When I was young, I had a relatively good income and a fantastic lifestyle, with a modest share portfolio and a small savings. And life was free and fun.

'When I turned thirty, I woke up with a shock. Looking back over those years, I had lots of fun and then suddenly I realised that I had not saved for my retirement. Yes, retirement seemed so far away at that age, however now that I am in my mid-sixties it just seems like yesterday.

What I did at the age of thirty was to estimate what I would need financially at retirement, and then I worked backwards to what I would need to start implementing from that day forward. I remember that in the beginning it looked like a wish list and seemed an impossible task at the time, but as I worked through the plan over the years it was not that difficult, and I did not have to make many sacrifices.

'I love my travel and, in those days, when my parents were alive, I would fly from Melbourne to Singapore just to visit them over the weekends. I loved eating out then with my friends and had a few favourite restaurants and I called them my "second kitchen".

I still went to the theatre, musicals, and live concerts. I had sufficient funds to entertain and hold parties and I decided I just could not imagine giving all these up in my retirement, and so these "fun and good times" had to fit into my financial plan as well.

'My worst fear then was to imagine going to a restaurant, looking at the menu and saying to myself: I cannot afford to have this particular dish, or that desert, and so on! It would be traumatic if I could not have my favourite dishes, or I was going to be living in a less than preferred lifestyle in my old age. That is not on. I was determined that I would not go backwards in life by spending my future. To me, that was not a good picture.

'Both my partner, Athol, and I live off our passive income from some shares and mainly properties.

'My mother would say to me "cash is king". If you have money in your old age you will have many "friends", and everyone will want to know you and help you. However, if you do not have money when you are old, you will have to suffer in silence because no one will want to know you or care for you. That is ironic but truthful, is it not? Looking back now, at some of the people I know, I recognise how true this is. Their children don't even want to visit them now in their old age. I find this rather sad and feel sorry for them. However, you now know you have a choice and knowledge to create your own life.

– Pearl Yeo

So, in working backwards and knowing what you want and need in your retirement, it is easier to establish a plan of action. When you are still young and working, it is easy to leverage on your assets; in particular, real estates or property. However, it is essential not to over stretch yourself because you still need to have a life and investments. You will build your wealth and yet be financially comfortable, allowing your tenants to help you pay the mortgage.

Many people tend to assume that if they work hard and save money then one day, they will end up wealthy. This is wishful thinking. With this mindset, they are more likely to end up with some modest but useful savings, and unlikely to be wealthy. Many people are rather 'risk adverse' and they invest only in a term deposit (if anything.) Interestingly, these people are the ones who said they 'live a simple life and don't need much'. And yet, they do not take holiday breaks or go away for relaxation with friends and family. And they do not want to eat out – of course, there is nothing wrong with not eating out.

Research shows, that not many people are thriving. They are not fulfilled in their lives, nor excited about the future. To tap into the workings of human motivation requires a new mindset, a new skill set, and a new habit – and it can take years.

The following are the basic principles I adopted, other successful people have adopted, and I know Andrew has adopted it toward creating a comfortable retirement which allows for travel, enjoyment of a better lifestyle, fun, and doing the things that better enrich our lives and lives of others.

Of course, you want to be rich, and you are entitled to have financial freedom, good health, happiness, and be able to spend your time and money in whatever way you want in your retirement. You could retire earlier and be happier, particularly when you have applied the basic rules.

The first step is to understand the basic rules of creating wealth

1. **The time value of money concept**
2. **Savings and the power of compound interest**
3. **Invest in yourself and cash generating assets**
4. **Knowing your new commodity is not your labour, it's your ideas**

Understand the time value of money concept

The key to financial prosperity is realizing the potential value of every dollar that you have in your hands and to think of cash as seed money – you can either eat it (spend it) or invest it (sow it).

In finance there is the concept that one dollar today is more valuable than one dollar a year from now. The reason for this is two-fold:

- First, a dollar will probably buy less goods and services in the future due to the destructive force of inflation.
- Second, if you have the dollar in your hands today, you can invest it and earn a return in the form of dividends, interest, or capital appreciation.

Savings and the power of compound interest

Savings

Frequently new investors ask how much they should be saving for investment. The question may at first appear to be straightforward, however, the answer is not so straightforward because it depends on many factors. For example, it depends on the age of the investor, their income, the risk profile, their lifestyle, and so on. And it depends on how much money and passive income they want to receive in their retirement. And we show you how to work all that out.

History shows that investing in a good profitable business and property are the best ways to generate income and grow your money. Therefore, it is essential to save money, so you have more money to invest.

It is essential to understand the difference between good debts and bad debts.

- Good debts are those that will grow in value over time. For example: house and property historically double in value in ten years if you purchase in the right area and the right type of property.
- Bad debts are those that depreciate in value from day one. For example: credit card debts, car, borrowed money for holidays, etc.

With a few notable exceptions such as good debts, debt is a form of bondage – a disease that enslaves the borrower. Therefore, you need to recognize that bad debt is a habit that must be broken.

Knowing what bad debts are, the next step in building your wealth is to develop a plan to pay down high interest credit card debt. The credit card debt is probably the highest interest charged by any institutions.

Being free of bad debts and owing nothing

Imagine how your life would be without owing anything. You would own your car, own your house, you would have paid for your education, and you would be proud that you did it all yourself.

Like what you see? If you want to be financially free you will make it a priority to eliminate your debt quickly. However, say what you like, you need to seek a caring accountant who understands tax and investments to help you structure so that you can maximise your return. Remember: there are good debts and bad debts, and it is okay to have some debts, as long as you have positively geared investments in your retirement.

The Power of Compound Interest

Compound interest is interest paid on principal, and previously earned interest (or accrued interest.) Which means you can grow your principal faster.

Money is nothing more than a piece of paper with the image of a long-dead person on it. It is your understanding of the power of money and the value it represents creates wealth.

Once you understand the power and value of money it hasn't got a hold over you because you know it is derived from your relationship with it; you suddenly become free from the constant pressures and stress of worrying about it. This is because you learn how to appreciate money: you know its value, you know what it can do for you and you know how to manage it. If you do not know how to manage your money, money will control you.

In particular, you will put money away for ten, fifteen, or twenty years and not keep constantly worrying how much there is. Instead, you simply make sure that you consistently and regularly contribute to the savings to increase the pile of money for your future. You will reach a point where you have a neat amount that is sufficient to invest. In that way you reduce your stress of thinking you never have enough money.

When you commit to saving money, you may notice yourself falling into the trap of spending an extra $5 here or there because you think, 'It's not that much. I'll never miss it.' However, this is a huge mistake, and you soon appreciate why such small amounts are very significant when you apply the time value of money principle and the power of compound interest.

Remember not to disregard small savings or small amounts as they will grow for you over time.

Invest in yourself and cash generating assets

Centuries of research and real-life experience have proven that business ownership, property investments, and shares are the best asset classes on an inflation-adjusted basis.

Historically the property value is said to double every ten years and is considered a stable investment if you buy right (i.e. buying property is about location, location, location – commonly, the right type of property in the right location.)

And yet, you cannot begin to invest unless you have cash left over at the end of every month, which means you need to save. With a positive cash flow property, you still need cash for unforeseen circumstances, or any times between tenants.

With a saving habit, you will have cash to invest. When you invest in cash generating assets –such as buying an investment property – you have your tenant paying off your mortgage. When you buy shares with dividends that provide a reasonable return, you can reinvest the dividends to further help you to build your wealth. This will be less stressful because you will always have funds coming into your bank accounts, providing greater liquidity and flexibility, particularly in building your wealth when you are young resulting in cash flow in your retirement.

Shares are mentioned here in the context of it being a useful tool. A tool to be used by reinvesting dividends, to grow money, then – when you have sufficient capital – you could sell some of the shares as 'seed capital' for investing into property. You can later use the properties as leverage for the next property.

In order to create and build wealth it is crucial that you understand basic accounting, economics, and finance. You can either enrol yourself in a short course or do self-study.

The initial cost for the training may seem huge at the time, however the knowledge you gain can make a large difference to your income, because you learn and understand the principles of accounting and how to manage your money wisely. The initial outlay for your education is repaid many times over during the years of your investment life.

For example, with the proper training in accounting, economics, and finance, you learn the best ways of investing in shares over time by knowing the dollar cost average over a diversified group of shares or a low-cost index fund. You learn that by spreading purchases over time, as well as reinvesting the dividends; your money buys more shares with a lower average price.

Think of it this way. If you spend $1000 to buy a 'gadget' for the home, it may not make a lot of sense when you can sell it for only 5% or less at a garage sale.

However, if you spend the same money to buy an old coffee vending machine, for example, and place it in a busy office where people are going to be putting money into it every day to purchase a cup of coffee, it will not only retain its value (because you can always sell the machine as a going venture in the future) and it has also provided you with cash income over those years. It is like putting coins into your bank.

Say what you like, no one can learn investing skills quickly without help. It may be necessary whilst you are educating yourself to seek advice or services of some experts if you already have the funds and are ready to invest. This is particularly vital if you are time poor. I sincerely believe that you must feel comfortable with the service provider you select because he or she is the person whom you will be working with.

You must feel and believe you can trust that someone, and they must have integrity and have your interest at heart. There are many 'sharks' in the marketplace, and one needs to weed them out. You do not have time to waste with 'sharks'. This way you will learn a lot more about investments: where and what to buy to meet your requirements and own agenda. This way you can start your investment earlier and not waste your time and money.

Remember, no two people have the same needs and wants, and there is no one template that will suit everyone. At the end of the day only you, and you alone, will know what you want and what your requirements are.

Knowing your new commodity is not your labour, it's your ideas

Many people believe that they need to work hard to be wealthy. This is not the case nowadays because of technology. Many wealthy people started their own business from ideas they had, and it is no different these days. It is believed by many that it takes 'guts', 'courage', and 'perception' to set up your own business, especially when you do not know if it is going to work for you; giving up a regular pay cheque for an uncertain future is daunting.

However, you have a choice, and if the opportunity is there, you can always start your business part time, initially, until the business income can replace and give you more than your regular pay cheque.

Successful, wealthy people are not held back by negative, limiting beliefs. They are often positive in thinking and attitude and believe in themselves. They have a 'can do' outlook. Nothing is too difficult for them – they will give it a go.

They believe in abundance and believe that their ideas will work for them. They also learn from their mistakes, and pick themselves up, and don't beat themselves down. Wealthy people have a mindset that recognises opportunities around them and leverage off these to create more income.

In comparison, people with negative money mindsets often experience poor results.

They struggle to pay bills, and often get caught up in the drama of when are they getting the next pay cheque, and (as a result) are always waiting for the next payday. They fear debt and often believe they do not deserve better jobs. They cannot see opportunities and will turn down opportunities because they believe it is 'too easy' and, therefore, 'cannot be for real'. The 'why me' syndrome so often ends in dead-end jobs and these people need not have to face a bleak future. This is because such attitude is not cast in stone; they can change if they want to.

So you do not want to go into your own business, that's fine too. You have ideas you can also invest in shares and properties. Many people have also become wealthy through their investments in properties or shares (and most likely both.) Why not let your money work for you for a change, instead of always working for your money? This is what will happen when you start investing in your ideas, either in a business, in shares or properties, or in all of the above.

As we get older, many people yearn for the 'perfect day' in their retirement. How do you live a perfect day, day after day after day? Isn't that what everyone wants?

One exercise you can do is to imagine that we have only a few days left to live and imagine what you would like to do in the last few days if money is no object. Then create a bucket list. This can be a rather entertaining and fun exercise. The reality is that even if you end up with a perfect day, and if you do it day after day, it will become boring and it's a routine.

At the end of the day we need to wake up to reality and face the fact that to be wealthy and successful we need to earn money; we need to save, and we need to invest to grow our capital and create income. What we need is to have ideas; we need to believe in ourselves; be committed to our ideas; use our savings to explore and learn from any mistakes instead of blaming them on someone or something?

Ideas breed more ideas, and the more you are able to tap into your inner mind, the clearer you will see. You will notice that you have become more positive when you start to change. You can see the opportunities, and will have more ideas, and will know how to access to more funds for investments, etc.

No two people will have the same strategy – it may be similar, but not the same. Your future is in your hands and you need to own it. Be responsible for it so that you can enjoy the fruit of your labour, just as you intended it to be.

Life's strategy should not be a standard template. You and only you know what you want in your life and what future you seek. Do not allow anyone to talk you into a stereotype future, as this is your life. Take control. Own it, and take responsibility, as your future is in your hands. Don't look back and regret because now you know you have other options.

In conclusion, remember this: once you are able to tap into your inner mind, you will know how to leverage your mind – you will never find yourself in an 'impossible' situation. This is because your mind will always be able to 'see solutions' that others cannot.

If you are reading this, it is because you know you are ready to embrace your 'new life' and it is time for you to start your journey for transformation to be a happier, wealthier, and more successful you. This is your life and you have helped to create it the way you always intended it to be. No one knows it better than you. So start your journey now.

This section has been provided to help people to possibly move forward in life and not get trapped by procrastinating and self-sabotage. Counteract negative thoughts of 'cannot' by switching your mindset to 'yes I can' and be able to take positive action to move forward.

Pearl and Athol would like to thank Andrew Crossley for the opportunity of sharing our knowledge, our passion, and our experience with his readers.

Now you know everything is possible and you can do it.

'Come to the edge, he said. They said: We are afraid. Come to the edge, he said. They came, he pushed them … and they flew …'
– Guillaume Apollinaire

Final Word

You have almost come to the end of my handbook, and I am sure you have been able to take a great deal of benefit from having read my book. As the title suggests, there will be an updated version released in the future with any necessary changes, advances in methodology and action packed with more insights aimed at helping you start and/or continue to grow your portfolio. Property investing is a journey – it should be an enjoyable, stress-free journey, as should buying a house to live in.

The most important thing you could take away is balance. Without balance in a property portfolio, it will be difficult to grow a portfolio of adequate size to suit your future needs, without negatively impacting on the present and near future. We have to live life for today and live life with tomorrow in mind.

This book has been about what you need to do every time you purchase a any residential property.

About the Author

Growing up in Melbourne, Andrew Crossley left Australia at 20, he became an Austrian qualified ski instructor, which he worked as for several seasons. Later also becoming a qualified scuba diving instructor. He went on to work in the UK for a prestigious investment firm dealing with share market investors. In 1996, at the age of twenty-four, he was headhunted and moved to the Netherlands to work for a private equity firm. For eight years he dealt with high net-worth clients, handling investments in venture capital projects, international property funds, IPOs and off-market derivatives.

A relocation to the Cayman Islands and Italy followed, before arriving back in Australia in 2005. Experiencing prejudice (as many expats do) from most recruitment companies in Melbourne, one common theme emerged: his overseas qualifications and experience didn't particularly count in Australia. Disappointing: yes; a deterrent to success: no!

Drawing strength from completing three master's Degrees — an MBA, a Master of Commerce, and Masters of Commercial Law, obtaining an advanced diploma in financial services (financial planning), diploma in finance (mortgage broking management), becoming a licensed estate agent (Victoria, QLD and NSW) and a qualified property investment advisor (QPIA). Australian Property Advisory Group (APAG) was established (a buyer advocacy and property advisory business) in 2012. Then in 2021, established a mortgage broking business.

Andrew Crossley lives in Melbourne and is the #1 best-selling and award-winning author of twelve books.

- *Property Investing Made Simple*: 1st Edition 2014
- *Property Investing Made Simple*: 2nd Edition 2019
- *Property Finance Made Simple*
- *The Australian Property Investment Handbook 2019/19*
- *The 100k Property Plan*
- *Commercial Property and Residential Development Made Simple*

Including 6 books in the Billy and Harry Adventures children's book series.

APAG's buyer advocacy services specialise in working with investors and people looking for a place to live, from around Australia, to reduce risk, improve potential and take the time and stress out of each property purchase.

This is achieved through thorough research leading to the shortlisting of 'where to buy', sourcing of investment grade properties (the 'what to buy' to rent easily and remain in demand) and negotiation.

Negotiating on a client's behalf, can improve the chances of obtaining the property at a better price than what a client could do themselves, leading to a greater chance of the buyer's advocacy service being cost neutral.

Andrew's mortgage broking business under the banner of www.Austpag.com.au enables him to assist clients in reviewing their existing mortgage endeavouring to achieve a better interest rate, more favourable loan fees and benefits, and providing finance solutions for all residential and commercial property needs.

APAG was a finalist in the Australian small business awards of 2016. Andrew was highly recommended in the Investor Choice awards 2015 in the categories of Property Investment

Advisor and Buyer's Agent, was national runner up in the prestigious Readers' Choice awards of 2015 and recognised in the top 10 Property professionals in Australia by The Property Investor Magazine 2017. All his books became #1 best sellers on Amazon.

His book 'Property Investing Made Simple' won the coveted title of best book: in 'Real Estate' International book awards 2015 and 'Real Estate' Book excellence awards 2016. 'Property Finance Made Simple' and the 'The Australian Property Investment Handbook 2018/19'made it to #67 and #68 respectively out of all books on Amazon Australia

Andrew, having worked in the finance industry, concurrently with managing APAG, became a multi award winning Business Development Manager helping mortgage brokers who were his clients, to structure mortgage finance for their clients.

Finance Industry Awards include:

- NATIONAL WINNER: Australian Mortgage Awards (AMA) 2018
- NATIONAL WINNER: Mortgage and Finance Association of Australia (MFAA) 2017 STATE WINNER: MFAA; 2017, 2020

- Finalist: Better Business awards 2017, 2018, 2019, 2020, 2021
- Finalist: MFAA; 2014, 2015, 2016, 2017, 2018, 2020, 2021
- Finalist: AMA; 2015, 2016, 2018

Andrew has also written for dozens of industry and non-industry publications and appeared on several TV and radio programs, and is an educator, mentor, consultant and public speaker.

Personal Message:

This blueprint is a step-by-step process that I personally take my clients through when I am engaged to assist in the capacity of a buyer's agent and property advisor.

I am sure you will enjoy reading my book as much as I have enjoyed writing it and sharing my knowledge and insights with you. Whether buying your first home/investment property or your next, it should be a worthwhile and enjoyable experience.

'If you have knowledge,
let others light their candles with it.'
— **Winston Churchill**

Contact

If you would like assistance with buyer advocacy, property advice or a mortgage, or being put in contact with a suitably qualified professional offering one of the other services of those listed in chapter 7, please contact us.

RESOURCES

The 'readiness to invest questionnaire', my blueprint to Property Investment Success ©, the comprehensive research checklist *or purchase one of Andrew's other books, go to the following link.* please visit my website.

www.australianpropertyadvisorygroup.com.au/resources

ONLINE COURSE

I have developed an online course; this is a cost-effective way in which you can drastically enhance your knowledge.

https://bit.ly/3GIbD6U

EMAIL
Buyer Advocacy and Property Advice

advice@australianpropertyadvisorygroup.com.au

Andrew@apag.com.au

PHONE
1300 760 901

WEBSITES

www.propertyinvestingmadesimple.com.au

www.propertyfinancemadesimple.net.au

www.australianpropertyadvisorygroup.com.au

www.facebook.com/
australianpropertyadvisorygroup

www.facebook.com/
propertyfinancemadesimple/

www.facebook.com/
Propertyinvestingmadesimple/

www.twitter.com/CrossleyAndrew

https://www.linkedin.com/in/andrewccrossley/

https://www.instagram.com/andrewccrossley/

Printed in Australia
AUHW020624061222
372122AU00018B/18

9 781922 691552